Mustard
Seed
Shavings

Text copyright © Steve Tilley 2011
The author asserts the moral right
to be identified as the author of this work

Published by
The Bible Reading Fellowship
15 The Chambers, Vineyard
Abingdon OX14 3FE
United Kingdom
Tel: +44 (0)1865 319700
Email: enquiries@brf.org.uk
Website: www.brf.org.uk
BRF is a Registered Charity

ISBN 978 1 84101 828 7
First published 2011
10 9 8 7 6 5 4 3 2 1 0
All rights reserved

Acknowledgments
Unless otherwise stated, scripture quotations are taken from the Holy Bible, New International Version, copyright © 1973, 1978, 1984 by International Bible Society, and are used by permission of Hodder & Stoughton Publishers, a member of the Hachette Livre UK Group. All rights reserved. 'NIV' is a registered trademark of International Bible Society. UK trademark number 1448790.

A catalogue record for this book is available from the British Library

Printed in Singapore by Craft Print International Ltd

Mustard Seed Shavings

Mountain-moving for beginners

Steve Tilley

Contents

Introduction

I am a vicar, of sorts. It's a bit more complicated than that, but don't worry for now. I have been working for various churches and Christian organisations for 25 years. Some days, wearing a dog collar, I look at myself in the mirror and think, 'No. How did that happen?'

But it did. And the fact that it could happen to someone like me, and that, by God's grace, I could make a go of it, is as close as I can get to an argument for the existence of God. How else could it have worked?

What about you? I'm assuming you are reading this because you are happy to be identified as a Christian. Perhaps it's a recent decision and someone has given you the book. Maybe you have been a Christian for some time but have never really worked through the implications your faith has for your life. Maybe you liked the cover. Maybe you don't know why, but somehow my text and you are in the same place. There's something going on in your life and it's slightly out of control. Feels like that, anyway. I like you already.

If writing, as Bill Bryson says, is a way of communicating across time, then my study in March 2010 and you, wherever and whenever you are, have now met. Brilliant, and hello. If you are nosey about me, the author, I blog at http://stevetilley. blogspot.com. I tweet as s1eve. (The second symbol is the numeral 1.) Pop in and comment, or follow.

Jesus said that faith the size of a mustard seed could move mountains. I haven't moved any, yet, so my faith must be smaller, but it's a starting place.

Anyway, trying not to sound too arrogant, this is the book I never got to read. It is also the book many others never got to read. When I took the decision to be a follower of Jesus in 1975, all the written help I got was either too holy (I never felt even close to achieving the standard) or in the 'worthy but dull' category, which I simply couldn't get through. Apologies to all you lovely Christian authors who tried your best. You weren't for me. I know you changed the lives of many others. Respect.

I've been encouraged by friends who had similar experiences to mine to try and produce an entertaining, punchy guide to hearing God. There are ten chapters. They follow, roughly, the themes of the Ten Commandments but do not give you a bunch of rules.

'Rules'? School rules? It's the rules? House rules? The word has a load of baggage if it's a noun. But if it's a verb?

Life is good. Life is precious. Life is special. Life rocks? Life rules.

That's better. Can you feel the pressure dripping off?

Life Rules was going to be the title of this book for a while, but I felt unhappy with the word 'rules' anywhere on the cover. Christianity is far more like receiving a present than a set of rules. So it became a book about learning to begin to think as a Christian—picking up the basics. One day, that mountain will move.

Many people have suggested to me that they wished they'd been told how hard the Christian life was going to be, before they set out. If that's you and you're reading this book as a refresher of sorts, I want to encourage you to keep going. Life can be hard. Cruel, even. If you are facing it as a Christian, you do not have the privilege of making a comparison with what life would be like without your faith. I'd suggest making the assumption that it might be every bit as difficult, if not worse. And, in case the first shadow of a call to full-time Christian work has appeared in your eye-line, I want to tell you it can be hard but it is also full of joy, job satisfaction and variety. A character in Terry Pratchett's book *Small Gods* says, 'It's indoor work with no heavy lifting.'

Don't panic if you are committed to Jesus and have, as yet, no idea what that will mean.

A friend of mine once announced that he had decided to eliminate hurry from his life, ruthlessly. I invited him to consider if it might be a job best done slowly. I can be a very annoying friend. Walk gently with me into the Christian life and let's explore together. Becoming a Christian has some implications. Let's work through them. Ambling, not running.

At the end of each chapter is a pause for thought, followed by a couple of discussion questions and a brief prayer. I hope it helps.

My thanks to Naomi Starkey for her guidance as we planned the book and the text took form—also to Lisa Cherrett and her team for managing the project into life and the words into order. And a strange sense of gratitude to a printing machine operator in Singapore I will never meet, who, in this amazingly connected world, worked with us to make it happen.

All the royalties from this book will go to The Trinity Project, an imaginative programme to restore an old rectory for the good of the local community in Nailsea. The better the book sells, the more generous I will have been.

Me and my Bible

Christians get their primary information about God from the Bible, and the Bible starts at the book of Genesis in a garden called Eden.

What's historical and not historical in scripture? It's a struggle to find out, and not always obvious. The Bible is a story—sometimes a historical account, sometimes not—about God and how people have understood him and his working in the world down the ages. It is 66 books, not one, but it makes a single collection. The books are a range of different types of writing, from letter and poem to historical journalism and drama.

I have written more about my personal understanding of the Bible at http://stevetilley.blogspot.com/2007/01/archive-stuff.html.

If you want to dig deeper into this scholarly debate, get hold of some of the work by the excellent and readable Karen Armstrong. Her latest, *The Case for God*, is published by Bodley Head (2009) and the second chapter is about how understandings of God have developed over time.

The pattern for the book you are about to read is going to be provided by the Ten Commandments. They were delivered at a particular time and in a particular place.

Whilst I believe that the first eleven chapters of Genesis have their origins in story rather than history, in chapter 12 we meet Abraham. The account of him, his son Isaac, Isaac's son Jacob (often called the Patriarchs) and Jacob's son

Joseph forms a historical foundation for the developing story of God and his people. God met with a particular person at a particular time and made a particular promise.

These people grew from a smallish, wandering, extended family to a gathering of people who eventually found themselves, because of famine, in the already developed nation of Egypt, a place where Joseph had a fine reputation. Here, though, they became slaves and captives when Egyptian leaders who knew nothing of Joseph came to power.

The book of Exodus is the story of Moses and God's call on his life to lead his people out of captivity into their own land. In the context of this journey, from slavery to wilderness wanderings to promised land, the Ten Commandments are given to Moses and written down.

We will find that the books of Genesis and Exodus are gripping narratives, whether or not we consider them historical literature.

I am certain that people will believe more about God if we confess that some of our stories are stories. Every now and again we can tell them a story that really is history. That empty tomb. You'll never believe it, but... As you read the Bible, you will be drawn towards one key truth, which you will be asked to judge as historical fact—the resurrection of Jesus Christ from the dead. It may be a matter that requires faith or a verdict based on evidence, but the Bible makes claims for the historical truth of the resurrection of Jesus that it doesn't make about other events, even his birth.

Read 1 Corinthians 15:1–19 to check this out:

If Christ has not been raised, our preaching is useless and so is your faith (1 Corinthians 15:14).

Those who find themselves in churches that take a conservative approach to the Bible will find me disappointing company. I'd love you to come with me anyway but I realise we will be seeing things in different ways.

To find out about God, read the Bible. One of the best Bible reading aids is a bookmark. Often, in our churches, we fool people into thinking that the Bible can only be read in ten-verse chunks. In some of our churches there is never any consecutive reading of scripture and a seemingly random set of passages is covered week by week.

My ordination put me in touch with the delights of the Anglican lectionary, whereby at Morning Prayer each day the Bible is read and, over a three-year period, the whole Bible is completed. When we meet for Morning Prayer at the church where I work, we leave a pause after each reading for thoughts and discussion. Nothing too long or too deep, but we allow the Bible to get to us, to get under our skin. The main thing is that we read it and let it soak into us day by day. I don't always get to Morning Prayer but I do keep up with the readings.

How might you do this if attending a weekday service is impractical? Many Christians are enthusiastic about the idea of a daily time to pray and read the Bible. They might call it a Quiet Time. It is a good discipline, but... here is one of those 'relax' moments. It is not necessarily biblical.

The Bible suggests that we 'pray continually' (1 Thessalonians 5:17).

The psalmist says he loves to 'meditate on it all day long' (Psalm 119:97b).

The Bible itself is more enthusiastic for our hearts to be God-centred than that we open the book for 20 minutes a day when there are other things we need to be getting on with. So why not enjoy the liberation of having a one-hour Quiet Time every three days, or five minutes twice a day? Your call.

Bible reading notes are made available by many Christian publishers, including the publishers of this book. Check them out at www.brfonline.org.uk or at a Christian bookshop or resources exhibition.

If you are reading this book, you are probably a bit booky. Research in the 1990s showed that 60 per cent of the population of the UK read one book a year or less. Being non-booky is not the same as being illiterate. It means that books do not come naturally to many people. So well done for getting this far, but the FSP version of the Bible (Fifteen hundred pages, Small print and Pictureless) may seem daunting.

Could you try listening to the Bible being podcast as you jog or walk the dog, or listening to a Bible study podcast on the web, your iPod or mobile phone? These ways are brilliant for a non-book culture:

- http://thebiblepodcast.org/podcast
- www.scriptureunion.org.uk/89157.id

Many churches have small groups that meet for mutual support, prayer and Bible study. Some Christians cultivate the habit of reading the Bible with a supportive friend, often in a mentor relationship. Book groups are popular these days and are a good way to make you read a book a month. Having to discuss a book holds you to account. You could belong to a Bible study group in a similar way, perhaps, meeting once a month to discuss your latest agreed reading plan.

I've dwelt on getting to grips with the Bible because I believe, with all my heart, that direct communication from God is always going to be imperfect. Not from his point of view but from ours. When we think we hear God speaking to us or giving us an image, it is going to require interpretation. The Bible is the best test of such communication that we can get.

Now we'll look at what God has said, as recorded in—yes, you guessed—the Bible.

Introduction to Part 1

Although the Ten Commandments are numbered 1 to 10, there is no suggestion that they are of decreasing importance. Nor is it true to say that they say all there is to be said about relationships. If we think of them in that way, we end up imagining Moses returning to the Israelites at the bottom of the mountain, with the Commandments written on tablets of stone, saying something like, 'OK, lads, I've got him down to ten but I'm afraid adultery is still in.' It wasn't like that. They are a starting point.

Jesus explained it better.

OK, said an expert in the law to Jesus one day, 'Which is the greatest commandment in the Law? (Matthew 22:36).

He probably meant which of the many instructions in the books of the Law (Genesis, Exodus, Leviticus, Numbers and Deuteronomy) was the most important, not simply if Jesus could put the Ten Commandments into an order of priority.

Whatever he meant, Jesus both answered his question and exposed his hypocrisy.

'Jesus replied: "Love the Lord your God with all your heart and with all your soul and with all your mind. This is the first and greatest commandment"' (Matthew 22:37–38).

Trying to organise the commandments into order exposes an attitude problem. As we read through them, and some of Jesus' commentary upon them, we discover that they are not so much rules as states of mind.

Jesus' answer to the expert in the law is taken from Deuteronomy 6:5. In other words, it comes from one of the books of the Law. It summarises commandments 1–4, which are all about our relationship with God. In commandments 5–10 we discover that our relationship with God has some implications for our relationships with our neighbour. (More on that in Part 2.)

It is no good knowing the law if it means nothing to you. It's like knowing the speed limit and driving as you please.

We are commanded to love God with heart and soul and mind. Can love be commanded? Can it be carried out thoroughly using emotions, spirit and brain?

Let's see.

1

It's me first, stupid

'I am the Lord your God, who brought you out of Egypt, out of the land
of slavery. You shall have no other gods before me.'
Deuteronomy 5:6–7

Not only is there no God, but try getting a plumber on weekends.
Woody Allen

There is a God. Or, to be clearer, there is God. Or maybe, to
have one last go at clarity, God *is*.

For since the creation of the world God's invisible qualities
—his eternal power and divine nature—have been clearly
seen, being understood from what has been made (Romans
1:20).

We should, this verse says, be able to look at the world and
deduce God's existence. Clearly. Unerringly. No confusion.
But we don't. So what went wrong?

The theologian Karl Barth said, 'God may speak to us
through Russian Communism, through a flute concerto,
through a blossoming shrub or through a dead dog. We shall

do well to listen to him if he really does so' (*Church Dogmatics*, 1948). But monstrous people have done outrageous things because they thought they heard the voice of God telling them to do so.

God is totally other. He is distanced from us. Trying to understand him is like looking at a blurred image, said the apostle Paul:

Now we see but a poor reflection as in a mirror; then we shall see face to face. Now I know in part; then I shall know fully, even as I am fully known (1 Corinthians 13:12).

If we want to know what God is like, the Bible tells us to look at Jesus:

He is the image of the invisible God, the firstborn over all creation (Colossians 1:15).

The Son is the radiance of God's glory and the exact representation of his being (Hebrews 1:3a).

I am a Christian because of Jesus. The writer Brian McLaren puts it this way:

I am a Christian because I have a sustained and sustaining confidence in Jesus Christ.
BRIAN MCLAREN, *A GENEROUS ORTHODOXY* (2004)

Where do we find out about Jesus? In the Bible.

Finding out about God will involve working at it. Living with him in mind. Tuning in to him. Becoming aware of him. It won't be straightforward. Please don't let anyone tell you it might be simple. If they already have, put that thought out of your mind again, please. Finding out about God means grappling, in some way, with the contents of the Bible.

Karen Armstrong says, 'There is no clear, consistent image of God in Genesis' (*The Case for God*).

Karen is right, but her writing suggests that this might be a negative thing. In fact, it is tremendously positive. If our human understanding gave us one clear and easily graspable picture of God, then that God would not be essentially 'other' but simply another version of us. So our Bibles show us God who is a warrior, leading his people into battle, telling them to be bold and strong. They give us God who reveals himself partially in dreams, visions and insights; God who wants to mother his people like a hen cares for its chicks; God who wants his prophets to live out ghastly, real-life metaphors by cooking on excrement or marrying prostitutes to show how he feels about his people; God who is intimate and distant, caring and angry, enthroned on high and surrounding his people, the house builder and the house occupant. There are even books of the Bible in which God makes little or no appearance, yet is a backdrop to all that is going on. Which of these is the true picture? All of them. Together.

It is not easy to 'see' what God is and there are no simple answers to life's perplexities.
KAREN ARMSTRONG, *THE CASE FOR GOD*

Whilst the Bible is, I believe, inspired by God, in it we see human words describing people trying to make sense of the seemingly random way life works out.

Perhaps God did not, we may find out one day, prefer Abel to Cain, or Jacob to Esau, but that is the way it looked to the people who were trying to do their theological writing between 950 and 400BC, when the text of Genesis was being assembled. Their insights are sacred, God-breathed and, of course, culturally stranded in a different time and place. It is not easy, but it is amazing, awe-inspiring and delightful to try to 'get' God.

Jesus was once asleep in a boat when a storm blew up (see Mark 4:35–41). The disciples were anxious and asked him, 'Teacher, don't you care if we drown?' (v. 38b).

He did care. He rebuked the wind, which calmed, and he rebuked the disciples, who were, presumably, embarrassed. Sometimes it feels as though God is asleep when we pray. He isn't, but it can feel like that.

Sometimes God doesn't speak. Our expectation of normal Christian life might be a little better if we recall the opening to the great calling of the prophet Samuel:

In those days the word of the Lord was rare; there were not many visions (1 Samuel 3:1b).

Samuel had to be taught to listen. When the word of the Lord did come to him, he thought it was Eli the priest speaking from across the room.

So, to revisit the commandment quoted at the beginning of this chapter, how do we go about putting God first? Here's another moment when I invite you to chill a little. I have often heard well-meaning preachers suggest that God should go at the top of a list of priorities which runs something like this:

1. God
2. Family
3. Church
4. Job
5. Friends
6. Hobbies

This is a thing that has bugged me ever since I originally heard it—firstly because points 2–6 on the list might vary quite a lot. If I see an old lady fall over in the road, I will not leave her there because I am on the way to pick up my kids from school. And sometimes—get this—I do put my church work ahead of my family. They have agreed to this and they understand, because they are nice people. A decision to be ordained is a decision never to be able to drop everything and go off for the weekend. Ever. I knew that when I signed up. But that's not the big problem with this list.

The big problem, for me, is that God is on the list at all. If he is totally other, transcendent and beyond, then he isn't so much on the list as before the list. It is a bit like putting 'breathing' at the top of the list. If I stop doing that, I'm in a mess. It is a given, not a priority. That's how I feel about God. He *is*, as I said before. And if he *is*, then a God who ends up on a list of priorities at all, even at number one, is too small.

Discovering that there is a God, whom the Bible speaks about, a God who wishes to communicate with us, is like having a new friend to share ideas and decisions with. It's a new relationship that needs nurturing. When I met my best friends, I didn't rewrite my priority list to include them. I took them on board (and they, me) and lived my list with them alongside me as new supporters and journey-sharers.

A number of books have been written against the idea of God in the last few years. Richard Dawkins' *The God Delusion* (2006) and Christopher Hitchens' *God Is Not Great* (2008) spring to mind. They are anti-faith polemic. Disciples of these two men even went to the trouble of putting adverts on the sides of buses saying (in an incredibly bet-hedging way), 'There's probably no God...'

They have made religious discussion a thing to do in public again, which is kind of them. The trouble is that the god they rubbish, I want to rubbish too. The god they rubbish ekes out a living in the gap between scientific understanding and things that still need to be understood. The god they rubbish apparently commands followers to fly planes into buildings. The god they rubbish refuses blood transfusions for his people. I think that sort of god is rubbish, too.

Listen to this:

God for Christian theology is not a mega-manufacturer. He is rather what sustains all things in being by his love, and would still be this even if the world had no beginning.

God is the reason why there is something rather than nothing...

Not being any sort of entity himself, however, he is not to be reckoned up alongside these things, any more than my envy and my left foot constitute a pair of objects. God and the universe do not make two.

TERRY EAGLETON, *REASON, FAITH AND REVOLUTION* (2009)

God is not on the list.

'No other gods before me'? Does that mean there are other gods but you shouldn't worship them? Or that all other gods are perversions and deceptions and don't really exist? It seems a bit early to launch into the 'Do other religions lead to God?' question, because the answer to that is usually nuanced with sensitivity and tact towards other faiths, and with one eye on Jesus' words in John's Gospel: 'I am the way and the truth and the life. No one comes to the Father except through me' (John 14:6).

The question is, why do you care? If you are not in touch with anyone of any other faith, why worry about it? You know Jesus as the way and that's good enough. If you do know people of other faiths, try listening to them. If they ask you about your faith, explain how it works for you. Congratulations! You're having interfaith dialogue. Pray that God will reveal himself to the other person as he has done to you, and leave the results to God.

I have heard a story like this so many times:

I was brought up in a Christian family but I didn't really have a personal relationship with God. Then one day (reading my Bible, talking to another Christian, praying alone…) I suddenly came to a deep understanding of God's love for me. It moved me (almost) to tears and I felt a profound sense of joy and peace. From that day forward I owned my family's faith for myself.

Brian McLaren describes some people's understanding of God as 'a single, dominant Power, Mind or Will (with) a universe of dominance, control, limitation, submission, uniformity, coercion…' (A *Generous Orthodoxy*).

Our understanding is that God is more intimate and relational than that. He meets with people, corporately and individually.

Moses' first direct experience of God was an interview in which God spoke from a bush that was on fire but did not burn up (Exodus 3—4). God refused to answer questions such as 'What shall I call you?' He simply gave his name as 'I am.' God is.

Our response needs to be a step of faith, deciding that we will walk with this God who is, even though sometimes the image is blurred. Sometimes he seems asleep in the boat. Sometimes we want words and visions and he is silent.

Shadrach, Meshach and Abednego were sentenced to die in a fiery furnace for refusing to bow down to the gods of the king in preference to the God who had revealed himself to them. How did they put their God first?

'If we are thrown into the blazing furnace, the God we serve is able to save us from it, and he will rescue us from your hand, O king. But even if he does not, we want you to know, O king, that we will not serve your gods or worship the image of gold you have set up' (Daniel 3:17–18).

'Even if he does not…'

Take a moment to consider what having 'no other gods before me' might mean.

'Even if he does not…'

Confessing Jesus as Lord means joining his revolution of love and living in this revolutionary way.

BRIAN MCLAREN, *A GENEROUS ORTHODOXY*

Plumbers do exist at weekends. They just don't come cheap.

Pause for thought

Any attempt we make to pin God down to an understandable form will fail. He is bigger than all our efforts to box him.

Discussion questions

1. Talk about your picture of what God is like. Has this chapter changed it at all?
2. What could God ask of you?

Prayer

Lord, I'm listening and looking. Reveal yourself to me.

2

Idol threat

You shall not make for yourself an idol in the form of anything in heaven above or on the earth beneath or in the waters below. You shall not bow down to them or worship them; for I, the Lord your God, am a jealous God, punishing the children for the sin of the fathers to the third and fourth generation of those who hate me, but showing love to a thousand generations of those who love me and keep my commandments.
Deuteronomy 5:8–10

The effort of coming to terms with things you do not understand makes them all the more valuable to you when you do grasp them.
Paul Arden, *The Independent* Media weekly, 3 October 2005

One of the smaller advantages of being a Christian is that it tends to put us into a place where we desire to learn. Learning new skills keeps us alive. It keeps our brains zippy and neurologically stops us from becoming stuck in a rut.

If you are very new to the Christian faith, you are likely to be making your brain healthier as you allow yourself not to 'conform any longer to the pattern of this world, but be transformed by the renewing of your mind' (Romans 12:2a).

That's good, isn't it?

Still, the commandment above sounds a bit heavy-handed,

doesn't it? The God who, later, is going to suggest that we don't covet (which seems to exclude envy as a behavioural trait) describes himself as a jealous God. Research needed. Is God a hypocrite? Why is God so anti-idol? And are we, as Paul Arden suggests, willing to devote the effort and energy to grasping this idea?

The word 'idolatry' has a Greek term, *eidos*, at its heart. It can mean 'visible form' or 'outward appearance'. So an idolater is anyone who tries to make the invisible God appear in visible form. Once upon a time, this meant building representations of him—models, statues and so on.

We need to pop back to Genesis, specifically 1:27. When the writers of Genesis were searching for a word to describe humans made in the likeness of God, there were many Hebrew words they could have chosen. The one they did choose is more often used to mean 'idol' than 'image' or 'likeness'. Humans were made to be God's idol. In an environment where the followers of other religions worship carved images of their gods, humans are told that they need no idol.

Why? Because they are the idol.

I recall reading this:

Always be prepared to give an answer to everyone who asks you to give the reason for the hope that you have (1 Peter 3:15).

It made me think. The suggestion in this verse is that I should expect to be asked about my faith. It should be normal. But nobody did ask. Then the penny dropped. If I do not live as one who appears different, who has a hope that others do not have, no one will be interested in asking.

Although it happens rarely, I heard the other day, via

another parishioner, that someone who was not a believer had said they might be willing to attend the sort of church I led. It doesn't happen very often but it meant that, for at least one person, something different and, hopefully, attractive had been seen in me.

If people want to know what God is like, then looking at humans should give them an idea. This has great implications for our behaviour. If you have recently become a Christian, you have taken upon yourself the responsibility of being God's idol—of representing God to others. How about that for a jaw-droppingly demanding job description?

It will happen to you, too. If you begin to make yourself known as a Christian in the workplace, at home or among your neighbours, people will want to try to catch you out. Hypocrite-spotting is one of the great leisure activities of the third millennium. Gossip magazines, columns and shows would have no content if they couldn't find celebrities behaving badly.

As a Christian, your behaviour will be under more scrutiny. Your language. Your manners. Your attitude. They're all being watched now. Because you exist to show others God.

This explains why later Old Testament writers were so sarcastic about those who did carve images of their gods. See Isaiah 44:9–20, for example:

[Idols] know nothing, they understand nothing; their eyes are plastered over so they cannot see, and their minds closed so they cannot understand (Isaiah 44:18).

If we bow down to, or worship, any representation of our God, we are, in effect, suggesting that the pinnacle of his creation is insufficient. We are saying, 'Don't look at us; look at this thing.' It's not, of course, that we should worship each other, either. We are flawed representations, but better than any hand-made idol at showing what God is like.

(I am grateful to theologian Dr Crispin Fletcher-Louis for these insights, delivered at a seminar at New Wine South West, 2008.)

In the time of the New Testament, the apostle Paul got upset about all this. In Athens, he was 'greatly distressed to see that the city was full of idols' (Acts 17:16).

Do we see this today? Temples and shrines of some other faiths are full of depictions and representations of the gods of those faiths. But do Christians do it? Here's one view:

The term (idolatry) can be understood to refer to any attempt that would render the essence of God accessible, bringing God into either aesthetic visibility (in the form of a physical structure such as a statue) or conceptual visibility (in the form of a concept, such as a theological system).

PETER ROLLINS, *HOW (NOT) TO SPEAK OF GOD* (2006)

Heavy stuff, but let's grapple with it. Pete Rollins seems to be saying this: any attempt to pin down God, either in a statue or a form of words, will be inadequate.

Karen Armstrong writes:

The crusaders' God was an idol; they had foisted their own fear and loathing of these rival faiths on to a deity they had created in their own likeness and thus given them a sacred seal of absolute approval.

THE CASE FOR GOD

So if we idolise a cause, a particular movement's theology or a single style of worship, or if we make ourselves disciples of a solitary Christian teacher, we run the risk of pinning God down in a way he will not be pinned. In the Bible, we are:

... presented with a warrior God and a peacemaker, a God of territorial allegiance and a God who transcends all territorial divides, an unchanging God and a God who can be redirected, a God of peace and a God of war, a God who is always watching the world and a God who fails to notice the oppression against Israel in Egypt.
PETE ROLLINS, QUOTING AN UNPUBLISHED ESSAY BY PHILIP HARRISON

The Bible does not want us to fix our theology in the current year and never move on from it. For the Jewish rabbis, the act of discussing, musing upon, meditating on and weighing up scripture was, and still is, as scriptural as the words themselves. It is in doing this that we find the Bible is alive. Understandings, forms of words and theologies that stand us in good stead at one stage in our lives may well get consigned to the dustbin later.

The Bible understands this. In Proverbs we read:

Do not answer a fool according to his folly, or you will be like him yourself. Answer a fool according to his folly, or he will be wise in his own eyes (Proverbs 26:4–5).

There are some things in life that are paradoxical, and scripture acknowledges this by putting two opposite teachings next to each other. Sometimes you can't win. Beware of worshipping the perfectly formed creed.

Lord Robert Winston, Professor of Science and Society and

Emeritus Professor of Fertility Studies at Imperial College, was discussing on the radio how so much of the peer-reviewed work he has written over his lifetime has turned out to be wrong. He was being overly humble. His work was 'wrong' only in the sense that people have built new understandings on the foundations of old ones. He meant 'inadequate'. He was introducing his new book, *Bad Ideas*. Our drive to invent and understand the world around us will lead to some incomplete ideas along the way.

Our desire to understand and speak of God will also lead to some clumsy words on the way to truth, because:

When we contemplate God we are thinking of that which is beyond thought; when we speak of God we are speaking of that which cannot be contained in words.

KAREN ARMSTRONG, *THE CASE FOR GOD*

I spend a lot of time in the Christian blogosphere, dipping into the sites of ordinary Christians, by and large. There are some lovely, kind and generous people out there. Every now and again, I come across a few more assertive sites. These are places where people, with unbridled verve and passion, denounce the unbridled verve and passion of other Christians.

Watch out for those who insist that their party line is the absolute corrective to all other sorts of Christian thinking. I don't go quite as far as Brian McLaren, who said that he was more interested in conversation than conversion. There is a point at which turning to Christ needs to happen. That is often after the conversation has finished. But the appalling arrogance of some of the people who say they 'love the gospel' shocks me, regularly. I often wonder if they love the people to whom they are preaching it.

As you embark on your Christian life and desire to be a seeker after truth (which I hope you will), go gently, listen carefully, question regularly and look forward to the day when the new heaven and new earth will do away with all our need to articulate theology.

At its heart, the commandment to steer clear of idolatry is an instruction to avoid any idea of having God taped. He is unknowable.

Often, though, discussion of this commandment turns to the question, 'So, what things do you put in the place of God? Do you worship your car? Your hobby? Your job? Your partner? Music? Computer games?'

While this is a good question, it is a different order of problem from that envisaged by the writer of Deuteronomy. We may spend a lot of time—too much time, even—on our personal activity (or inactivity) preferences, but that doesn't mean they are being treated as images of God. We need to pull the plug on the great guilt-trip which tells us that everything we do apart from prayer and Bible study is a waste of time. Deuteronomy saw tribes and races building gods and then worshipping them. In the light of the special knowledge of God that the Israelites had received, they knew this was wrong and they set out their realisation as a commandment.

That said, is there a line in the sand? Are there aspects of human behaviour that, while not directly compromising our relationship with God, compromise our witness to him? Things that make us look less like the idols we are meant to be?

What about movies, sport or online activity? The magazines we read? The music we listen to? Can these things ever be deemed idols?

Only if we worship them. They can rob us of our time. They can lead to addiction. But that is not the same as idolatry. We might not want to be too black-and-white about time commitments, either. Anyone who became a leading expert on anything, from a football free-kick specialist to someone who catalogued the complete insect life of a suburban garden, got there by spending an inordinate amount of time on their subject. We might like to be generous towards the compulsive personalities of those who were addicted to finding cures for heart disease, making foolproof soufflés or perfecting virus-free computer operating systems.

Some people are very fond of reminding us that, as Christians, we are 'in the world but not of it'. What on earth does that mean?

It has its roots in the otherworldliness of Paul, who said, 'Our citizenship is in heaven' (Philippians 3:20).

Over the years, many people have tried to restrict the behaviour of Christians. Sometimes the church can seem like nothing more than a way of controlling people. Movies, dance halls, alcohol, pubs generally, clubs and Sunday sport have all been biffed with the clunking fist of otherworldliness.

The joke going round a particularly strict Brethren community in the 1960s was that couples were not allowed to have sex standing up, for fear that it might lead to dancing.

I asked a diocesan youth officer colleague if he felt that there were risks attached to using a cathedral for a diocesan youth event. What would happen, I wondered, if the place got damaged? He told me that he was concerned, but he was more interested in young people learning to be holy than learning to be good. What better place than an ancient cathedral in which to begin to get in touch with God through an all-night vigil?

More important to be holy than good? Moses the murderer. David the adulterer. Peter the denier. Ring any bells?

Loads of things can get in the way of our prayer life. They are more likely to be distractions than idols, but we can counter their appeal by keeping our prayer and worship routine lively, on the move and vitalised.

There are many different ways and styles of communicating with God. It is worth exploring them all at an early stage.

Some churches will have a focus on spiritual gifts; words of knowledge, tongues and prophecy will be used in worship. Others will have a ministry to those who are unwell. Intercessions will always remember the sick.

Some Christians find that regular times of retreat are helpful. It is possible to stay a few nights in many monasteries, convents and retreat houses around the country. If you like a discipline of regular prayers (spoken or chanted), or an act of worship interspersed with periods of silence, this may well be for you.

I like space. With an old friend, I go away twice a year for three or four days to read, pray, think, share ideas and sleep well. It is a real tonic. Because I am paid to undertake a pastoral ministry, I can put this time down as work time. I get fed. Filled. It works for me. Find out what works for you.

Use the time or space to remind yourself of your responsibility to be a depiction of God to others. Refresh yourself so that you can point to God again.

The Bishop of Bath and Wells, Peter Price, in whose diocese I work, tells this story. 2009 was the 1100th anniversary of the founding of the diocese, and it was decided that Bishop Peter would walk the bounds of the diocese over a few months. He noticed this on his journey: as he spoke to groups of Christians, they wanted to talk about church, but as he chatted with groups of non-Christians, they were happy to speak of God.

Is it possible (and I say this as humbly and sensitively as I can) that we have made the church an idol? Are we are more interested in our buildings, our structures, our hierarchies and our systems than we are in God? I fear that might be the case.

What about shrines and places of pilgrimage? Lourdes? Walsingham? Do we substitute these places for God, saying that he can only work if we go there? In the same way, some people feel that God might be more present and available in a church building than in a home, and even more so in some parts of that church building than in other parts.

It doesn't help me personally very much, but visiting a shrine or place of pilgrimage, or viewing relics, is simply a way of accepting the psychological boost offered by praying in the presence of a physical reminder of someone who had a unique experience of, or communication with, God. The mists of time prevent us from knowing if there is a true historical event lurking behind the often over-the-top development of the shrine or pilgrimage site. We are simply being in the place where such an event may have occurred, and praying. It's not for me, but it's not bonkers and it is not idolatry.

I have to confess that there is something (I'm not sure what, but it isn't nothing) about praying in an old building where people have prayed for hundreds of years. I don't believe, as one dear churchwarden friend in the north-east said to me, that 'the prayers have soaked into the walls', but I love the way she put it.

A woman I was talking to last night said that she found being on the coast and looking at the sea a tremendous aid to prayer and faith. This woman had been through the death of a young husband and had found a place, and a way, that helped her pray. It helped her believe in God through the blackness. She was not worshipping the sea but allowing it to be a way of removing any distractions to seeing God clearly.

So, having said a lot about what not to do, I have to ask, how do we worship God properly and truly? Here are some Bible verses:

God is spirit, and his worshippers must worship in spirit and in truth (John 4:24).

Offer your bodies as living sacrifices, holy and pleasing to God—this is your spiritual act of worship (Romans 12:1b).

Although we read the word 'worship' in both these verses, we are reading the translation of two different Greek words. In the first one, from John 4, we are concerned with adoration, with giving God his true worth. It has the feel of a Sunday behaviour or a Quiet Time behaviour—words of truth spoken in the presence of the Spirit.

If you attend a church where a creed is used on a Sunday, the thought is that, as Christians gathering together, we are uniting around the agreed truth. The word 'creed' comes from the Latin *credo/credere*, meaning 'to believe'.

There are creedal statements in the New Testament. Philippians 2:5–11 is often thought to be one. The most common creeds used in churches today are the Apostles' Creed and the Nicene Creed. Their wordings were hammered out at a time when disagreement could lead to martyrdom, so seriously were they taken.

We need to remember that, when reciting a creed, we are doing our human best to make statements about God, using language that will always be an imperfect method for describing the Almighty. It may be good to look upon them as an agreed starting point rather than a finished article.

When we read about worship in Romans 12:1b, we are concerned with service, with worshipping God by serving him day by day. It is a reminder, again, to act as idols of God in everything we do. As one poet put it:

Who sweeps a room, as for thy laws,
Makes that and th' action fine.

GEORGE HERBERT, 'THE ELIXIR', 1633 (BETTER KNOWN AS THE HYMN 'TEACH ME, MY GOD AND KING')

I find it a help, personally, to recall that the same Holy Spirit who was present at creation, hovering over the surface of the waters (Genesis 1), who was uniquely present in Jesus and who inspired the Bible's authors to write their words down, can be with us as we read, as we live our lives and as we worship.

Dear children, keep yourselves from idols. (1 John 5:21)

Pause for thought

Don't be an idolater; be an idol.

Discussion questions

1. Ponder how you feel about your very life pointing others to God. Does that come with a weight of responsibility, or do you find it exciting?

2. Are there things in your life that have almost become idols, in the way they take your time or focus your thoughts? How could you get them back into true perspective

Prayer

Lord, help me to point others to you.

3

Flippity flip

'You shall not misuse the name of the Lord your God, for the Lord will not hold anyone guiltless who misuses his name.'
Deuteronomy 5:11

Modern life encourages the primitive and destructive side of all of us rather than helping us in the struggle to control these urges and resist these temptations.
Emma Klein and Judy Cooper, quoting an anonymous psychotherapist, 'Face to Faith', *The Guardian*, 21 May 2005

There are one or two books I have come across for which the title and jacket text summarised the message of the book so clearly that I got the point without needing to read it. *The Natural Touch: Reaching others for Christ* by Kim Swithinbank (1988) was such a book. I apologise to Kim that I was transformed by the title, not the text. The thesis I built on the title was that we had lost touch with discussing Jesus naturally. We had managed to make God-talk seem abnormal to such an extent that we were now embarrassed about it. How can we get normal, good use of the name of the Lord our God into conversations?

Too hard? Let's go back. How can we make sure our conversations are pleasant and people want to continue talking to us?

How about this? Try to speak politely. Try to be encouraging. Try to be slow to take offence or become angry. Try to cheer people up. Try to make them laugh, because laughter helps produce endorphins and they improve physical health. Try to be clear. The less well you know someone, the more you should avoid speaking in a roundabout way.

Now none of this ought to be on page 1 of a 'Becoming a Christian' manual. We all ought to do these things as a matter of course. It would make the world better. So why is it so difficult?

A plumber came to my office a few years back. He knew nothing of my faith or occupation. He found the defective valve in the heating system. When he announced that it was broken, of the five words he used, the first was 'The' and the following four were all F-word based—two adjectives, a noun and a verb. I understood him without a shadow of a doubt. That valve was beyond repair.

I have to say, I was not especially offended. As a minister, I am always more gratified than bothered when people do not adjust their language merely for my sake. I am not a habitual offender but would be fibbing if I told you I never swore.

What is swearing, anyway? For some people, it is merely the introduction of an adjective to give emphasis, especially when their vocabulary is limited. For others, it is simply a pause, like saying 'yes, no' at the beginning of an answer in order to gain time to think.

For yet others, especially the young, it is pretending to be grown up. 'Here are some words our parents say not to use. Therefore, using them must make you grown up,' they think.

Aged about seven, I asked my Dad what the writing on the swimming-pool cubicle wall meant. 'Daddy, what's a baster?' I could tell from his pause that I had now accessed a really good thing to say when I wanted attention (even if I hadn't got the word quite right).

For a fourth group, it's possible that they do not notice how riddled with poor language their conversation is. Swearing is the junk word string at either end of their conversational DNA... and sometimes in the middle, too.

Once, on being dismissed from a football field for directing foul and abusive language at the referee, the footballer Paul Gascoigne commented on the official, 'I wasn't swearing at him; I was just swearing.'

For the first few series, I was a fan of the TV programme *Changing Rooms*. Two sets of neighbours or friends took responsibility for redecorating a room in the other couple's home. Sometimes all was well, but I have to say the most entertaining programmes were those in which the hopes and aspirations of one couple, expressed, say, as, 'I'd be happy with anything so long as it isn't grey; I hate grey', were juxtaposed with shots of their room being redone in various shades of grey. You knew it was all going to end in tears. Friends and neighbours didn't seem to know each other nearly as well as they thought they did.

What I noticed about the language of the contestants was the first phrase uttered on viewing their newly decorated rooms. Three times out of four they would say, 'Oh (pause)... my God!'

It was neither a real expletive nor an acclamation, merely the contemporary way of expressing shock.

However, listen to any of several fly-on-the-wall documentaries following top-flight football managers around, and the expletive count hots up. Some are blasphemous, others merely crude. We seem a long way from the instruction to the Ephesian church:

Do not let any unwholesome talk come out of your mouths, but only what is helpful for building others up according to their needs, that it may benefit those who listen (Ephesians 4:29).

So even if we feel that an occasional expletive isn't the end of the world, we need to think of our listeners. The nature of any fairly large audience is such that it will include the offendable and unoffendable simultaneously. The expletive may not build everyone up.

It is complicated, though. Language moves on. You will find the word 'pisseth' in the 1612 King James Bible to describe urinating. When Paul counts everything as 'rubbish' compared to knowing Jesus (Philippians 3:8), any colloquial form of the word 'excrement' would be as good a translation as any other.

Listen to minister and teacher Trevor Lund on this subject:

As we give up words that are contrary to the will of God we need to replace them with words that we must say. This is a journey that requires the power of the Holy Spirit and sometimes a change in character.

That's OK. God wants you to mature. He wants you to grow more and more into the image of His son, who was the exact representation of the Father. Our words show us and others what's in our heart.

WWW.REVTREV.COM

Now all that may or may not be helpful to you, but life as a Christian involves getting a grip on your speech. The letter of James puts it thus:

The tongue also is a fire, a world of evil among the parts of the body. It corrupts the whole person, sets the whole course of his life on fire, and is itself set on fire by hell (James 3:6).

Welcome to a world where the words we speak to each other matter, more than they did before we decided to follow Jesus. What we say and how we choose to say it tells people who we are.

All I have said so far is commentary. It is an extension of later biblical understandings. The commandment itself is about a starting point. Remember, commandments are about minimum standards. We should do better than simply not misusing God's name. But how do we avoid that at all costs?

In the miracle of a burning bush that was not consumed by the fire, God revealed himself to Moses. Moses dared to ask what God should be called:

God said to Moses, 'I am who I am. This is what you are to say to the Israelites: "I am has sent me to you."'

God also said to Moses, 'Say to the Israelites, "The Lord, the God of your fathers—the God of Abraham, the God of Isaac and the God of Jacob—has sent me to you." This is my name forever, the name by which I am to be remembered from generation to generation' (Exodus 3:14–15).

Many fine words have been written since that day, concerning the names and titles of God in the Bible. For now, we need to be satisfied with this. God's name is special. So special that 'I Am' (in Hebrew, *Yahweh*) almost means 'the God with no name'. It is about what he will do and be rather than what he is called. And even that little word 'he' is confusing if we think God can be attributed with maleness in the same way that men can today.

This has left some Christians a bit mixed up. Overhear a group of Christians praying and you will hear them speaking to the Lord, their Father, Jesus, God and other titles as well.

It's not a big deal. We do not need to get our words right when we speak of God. The gift of the Holy Spirit is such that:

... the Spirit helps us in our weakness. We do not know what we ought to pray for, but the Spirit himself intercedes for us with groans that words cannot express (Romans 8:26).

What about when our guard is down, though? When we hit our thumb with a hammer or get cut up by another driver, or find our team's defence letting us down in the last minute, or fluff a putt, or drop the top off the salt as we add a little more to the pot? Then what? Does a name for God ever come out of your mouth at this point?

My only technique is to breathe in and count to three in my head.

I don't think it is worth becoming holier-than-thou when faced with others' misuse of our names for God. At the end of the day, we worship a God who can, if the Bible is to be believed, take care of himself, and will one day judge everyone in the world. Getting a reputation for having a Victorian style of disapproval at builders' language (no disrespect intended to builders) is not worth it. Smile back. And don't copy simply to show that you belong.

What, then, should we make of those who use different names for God? Is Allah God? Is Jah God?

The God I worship has said clearly that he is one. In the chapter after the Ten Commandments appear in Deuteronomy, we read this:

Hear, O Israel: the Lord our God, the Lord is one (Deuteronomy 6:4).

Jesus quoted this verse when answering the legal expert's question about which was the greatest commandment:

'The most important one,' answered Jesus, 'is this: "Hear, O Israel…"' (Mark 12:29a).

We are left with the conclusion that any other understanding of God is an incomplete revelation. There are not other gods, less powerful than the one we worship. There is one God, and a complete understanding of him is available only through Jesus Christ.

If someone calls you on this, try not to be defensive. Have faith in the transforming power of the gospel and tell them of Jesus, the one we have already discussed as the likeness of the invisible God:

In the past God spoke to our forefathers through the prophets at many times and in various ways, but in these last days he has spoken to us by his Son, whom he appointed heir of all things, and through whom he made the universe (Hebrews 1:1–2).

Tell your story and experience, which cannot be disputed. Talk of Jesus and your relationship with him. He completes the picture that is partially painted by other faiths.

The Christian faith enjoyed unique protection in the UK through the law against blasphemy until very recently (2008), although prosecutions were rare. The word 'blasphemy' comes from the Greek *blasphemo*, literally meaning 'to injure the reputation'. One thing you might feel about God by now is that he needs no help from us in protecting his reputation. Indeed, a sign of a mature and grown-up faith might be that it does not take attacks on its God too seriously.

I believe that people who say evil things about the Christian God usually do so out of ignorance rather than deliberate fault. When people do seem to set out to offend, however, be very wary about responding. Offences against our faith are best starved of the oxygen of publicity. Then they burn out. As soon as there is any public objection to some poor play, book, picture or programme, the media smell a story. The story is then not about the offensive item but about the row it has apparently caused. In talking up the disagreement, the offensive piece gets more publicity.

If you doubt this, simply consider the following:

- *The Satanic Verses* by Salman Rushdie
- *Jerry Springer, The Opera*
- 'Relax' by Frankie Goes to Hollywood
- Danish cartoons of the Prophet

These were all given a huge boost because someone, somewhere, tried to ban them. I rest my case.

In my last church, one of the leaders, an ethnically Asian woman, had a huge amount of respect for the Bible. She read it often and knew it well. She also kept one or two courtesies associated with being used to the company of Muslims, who respect and honour their holy books. For instance, if a Bible was on a low table in a staff meeting, she hated it if anyone rested their feet on the same table. She didn't like us to place Bibles on the floor. She saw it as a lack of respect for God's word.

Today, few of us keep such rituals. In most parts of the country, gone are the days when people dressed up to go to a church service. There are few Christian rituals associated with eating that are kept as a matter of course.

In the light of this, our non-ritual behaviour is all we have to draw people's attention to our faith: our words, our courtesy, even our manners.

We have to conclude that we are wise to be slow to take offence. The 'natural touch' is to allow our tales of God in our life—not a knee-jerk reaction to the absence of God in the lives of other people—to set the flavour of our conversation.

Pause for thought

Review the last few hours of conversation you have been involved in. Play them back over in your head.

Discussion questions

1. On balance, was your conversation 'building up' or 'tearing down' other people?
2. What steps do you think you could take to change the way you talk without compromising who you are?

Prayer

Lord, flavour my words sweetly, for one day I may have to eat them.

4

Pew fodder

Observe the Sabbath day by keeping it holy, as the Lord your God has commanded you. Six days you shall labour and do all your work, but the seventh day is a Sabbath to the Lord your God. On it you shall not do any work, neither you, nor your son or daughter, nor your manservant or maidservant, nor your ox, your donkey or any of your animals, nor the alien within your gates, so that your manservant and maidservant may rest, as you do. Remember that you were slaves in Egypt and that the Lord your God brought you out of there with a mighty hand and an outstretched arm. Therefore the Lord your God has commanded you to observe the Sabbath day.

Deuteronomy 5:12–15

The church of Jesus Christ should have all the flexibility of a movement, not the sterility of an institution.

Andy Hickford, in Pete Ward (ed.), *The Church and Youth Ministry* (1995)

It is fascinating that no commandment tells us to work but this one tells us specifically not to. Workaholics are a driven breed. They need to be reminded to stop.

Taking rest was a serious business in Israel. How often have you heard these verses?

Observe the Sabbath, because it is holy to you. Anyone who desecrates it must be put to death; whoever does any work on that day must be cut off from his people. For six days, work is to be done, but the seventh day is a Sabbath of rest, holy to the Lord. Whoever does any work on the Sabbath day must be put to death (Exodus 31:14–15).

Not often, I should wager. Still want to read those work emails on Sunday?

It is a while since TV and radio personality Noel Edmonds described going to church as the dullest experience available in the world, but he may still have a point. That's why it is important at this point to say that church is something you are, not something you do.

A cruel twist of nomenclature has meant that we call the building where the church meets 'the church', and so we talk about going to it rather than being it.

When people say that the church shouldn't get involved in politics, they usually mean that its leaders shouldn't speak out, not that Christians shouldn't vote.

People misunderstand the word 'church'.

How can we learn to be church? Being church is a job description. A mission. A task. An order. A calling. A belonging. It's not a once-a-week visit.

This commandment includes the word 'Remember…'. In one of many remarkable insights into serving God, my friend and colleague Bob Clucas once came up with this:

Vision is the ability to remember the purpose of the work.

FROM 'FRUIT', A TRAINING GAME, AVAILABLE FROM WWW.GODSTUFF.ORG.UK

I've never been able to improve upon that definition or find anyone else who can better it. Remembering what you are about is the key to working out where you are trying to get to.

So much of the Old Testament gives memory as the starting point for current behaviour. Take a day off, says the author, because once you couldn't. Take a day off, because you need to rest, whereas once you were slaves and worked all the time. Remember what that was like. Take a day off, because you need to worship. Remember when that wasn't possible. It took plague after plague and a Passover before Pharaoh's hardened heart released you to worship as you requested. Give your slaves a day off, because you remember what it was like when you were slaves.

In the list of commandments found in Exodus, the text is slightly different:

Remember the Sabbath day by keeping it holy. Six days you shall labour and do all your work, but the seventh day is a Sabbath to the Lord your God. On it you shall not do any work, neither you, nor your son or daughter, nor your manservant or maidservant, nor your animals, nor the alien within your gates. For in six days the Lord made the heavens and the earth, the sea, and all that is in them, but he rested on the seventh day. Therefore the Lord blessed the Sabbath day and made it holy (Exodus 20:8–11).

Remember the sabbath day. Take a day off, because the great stories of Genesis tell us that God did so in the very act of creation. He made everything in six days, then stopped. So should you. That's something else to remember.

The principles established by the two versions of this commandment have become somewhat separated over the years. It is good to take a day a week on which worship is the most important part of the day. It is equally appropriate to take a day every week on which rest is the most important part of the day. They can be the same day but they don't have to be.

At the end of each day of creation, God saw that what he had done was good, as he did when he rested on day seven. It's good to pause and reflect on what we've achieved before we rush on.

If you are a part of a lively church where you have duties on a Sunday, the day may not feel especially restful. You also need a break. Many Christian families see Saturday as their main day of rest or, at least, as a break from the normal routine of work; there are often household chores to be done. Then they gladly serve God in their local church in a variety of ways.

Why do Christians see Sunday as the usual day of rest? The Jewish Sabbath is the day we call Saturday, but Sunday became the Christian day of celebration because it was the day on which Jesus rose from the dead. But it is also about rest. The very root of the word 'sabbath' suggests 'cease' or 'stop'.

What should this 'day of worship' include?

Author Henri Nouwen listed five parts of a well-lived Christian life:

1. To dwell in God's presence.
2. To listen to God's voice.
3. To look at God's beauty.
4. To touch God's incarnate word.
5. To taste fully of God's infinite goodness.

QUOTED IN THE CPAS *GROWING LEADERS* COURSE

It seems to me that this writer has got a grasp of worship. These would be great constituent parts of a wonderful act of corporate worship (Christians getting together). I feel I would be more likely to get excited about 'going to church' if I had these five expectations. Why don't I?

I might struggle to give you a good answer to that. Take a small measure of English reserve, mix with a dash of less-than-perfect musicianship, add a drop of underprepared preaching and passionless intercession, break the boiler until the temperature is low enough and serve with disappointing coffee. Sorry. I'm delivering myself 20 lashes for cynicism as I write.

Sometimes I go to church services because of a sense of discipline. I always do it. It is my routine. On other occasions I go because of duty. I said I would, so I do. Always, it is the people I am with who make it worthwhile. Sometimes I go to support new preachers or worship leaders, or listen to people I mentor or train. Occasionally I go because I really, really want to. On those occasions, I know that God meets with me and would do so even if someone was reading from the Bristol telephone directory during a power cut.

I long, and try, to improve the churches at which I worship, especially the one where I am called 'Vicar', but the thing I love about my little church at Trendlewood is that the sense of family and community without cliquishness is second to none. We love to export leaders to ordination or other ministries. And the coffee is brilliant.

Our inadequate projection system has been a standing joke for three years, our worship leaders are all volunteers learning their trade, many of our preachers are also developing a new gift, so are not quite yet arena-fillers, and, as I write, many of our children's leaders have come to the conclusion that it is time to step down and we are praying hard for guidance as to how to proceed.

But this is church:

As you come to him, the living Stone—rejected by men but chosen by God and precious to him—you also, like living stones, are being built into a spiritual house to be a holy priesthood, offering spiritual sacrifices acceptable to God through Jesus Christ (1 Peter 2:4–5).

If it feels messy from time to time, that's because it is a place where building is going on. Ever seen a tidy building site?

However we might feel about getting together on a Sunday, it is good, and appropriate, to thank God corporately, if only for nothing less than another week's gift of life that we don't deserve.

I mentioned in Chapter 2 that two different Greek words are translated by the English word 'worship'. One is about adoration (more a Sunday word and a private prayer word). The other is about service, about offering 'your bodies as living sacrifices' (Romans 12:1).

In his Saturday *Guardian* column, Simon Hoggart is very scathing about those round-robin letters that people send at Christmas. Quite right, too. Some of them are dreadful. If you are on the receiving end, my only advice is that it is not rude not to read them. It is rude to send dull ones.

In February 2010, Simon Hoggart wrote this:

This is from a religious family, whose church work is well-rewarded. 'Tim works as an economist for a big music company. He earns lots of money, and lives in walking distance from the Oval cricket ground. God is good.' Later Tim's father goes with him to the Oval, in time to catch Stuart Broad take five wickets against Australia, 'putting England in an Ashes-winning situation. God is very, very good.' These people sound, in many ways, quite normal, yet they believe that God has arranged for their son to be rich, and for England to beat Australia. Puzzling, isn't it?

Well, no, Simon, if I may call you that, it isn't. Because that is not what the writer meant. There are many reasons why I am sure I would hate Tim's family newsletter but I have to defend the prose. It is the *Guardian* columnist who has assumed—wrongly, in my view—that thanking God for something good means believing he has arranged it. Believing in a God who is the maker and sustainer of the universe does involve remembering to thank him when things go well.

Have you noticed far more sportspeople crossing themselves as they run on to the pitch, or praising the heavens when they take a wicket or score a goal? There are some signs that people are living increasingly in acknowledgment that there is a God who cares and oversees.

I have a good life. I wouldn't be so presumptuous as to believe that every time I have an enjoyable evening, God has fixed it for me, like a divine Jimmy Savile, but I do thank God that it happened. It's a subtle distinction, but important.

Read the psalms. Hear the words of the hymn book of the ancient temple. These poets thank God when things go well and—get this—blame God when things go badly. They rejoice in the idea of banging their enemies' babies' heads against rocks, as well as in God's infinite love and patience.

None of this means that God is impressed by our thanks or our requests. If you ask for a scorpion, he may not give it. But it is important to be (and I can't avoid using a tired phrase) a 24/7 Christian. We need to live day by day in the light of God's overarching care and concern for us. That said, we also need to find a church community to which we can truly belong.

So, which church? That's complicated. Perhaps start at the nearest. Balance whether you feel you will be supported, taught and helped against whether you think you can fit in and help them. The church may have been praying for someone like you. There are many new ways of being church that are springing up. Fresh expressions. Online communities. Festivals and camps.

In my town we have a Roman Catholic church, a Baptist church, a Methodist church, a Free Evangelical chapel, a United Reformed church and three Church of England churches. Probably, children's initiation into the church and women's leadership would be the major theological stumbling blocks between us, but we tend not to talk about those things. We get on with ministering to the town in the name of the Lord Jesus. We do what we can agree about wholeheartedly. We meet together as leaders and ministers to pray once a month without fail. I would gladly tell a new Christian in my town to try any of these churches and see if it works for them.

Different church congregations show their emotions in different ways. Some will be quietly reverent, others more charismatically enthusiastic. I have no idea how emotional you are as a person. (By that, I mean I don't know how much it shows. We're all emotional.) But if you are led through life by your emotions, seek out movies that make you cry, feel the pain of others who suffer and, if they're not suffering, assume they are keeping their pain to themselves for no good reason, then hear this. You will probably be better served, and better able to serve, in a church where you feel emotionally involved rather than detached and out on a limb.

As an individual, you need to make an emotional commitment to God. You need to fall head over heels crazily in love with the person of Jesus—who he was, who he is, what he did and what he does. If you do this, you won't need a Christian lifestyle guide ever again. Simply stay in love; the rest is giftwrap.

I also don't know whether or not you like thinking. If you prefer the word 'what' to 'who', and if you prefer the word 'think' to 'feel', then you probably like thinking. Thinking not about anything in particular but thinking for its own sake—stretching your mind. You can probably tell by my title, stories, examples and illustrations that I love thinking. I don't really care what I'm thinking about; I like doing it.

Being a Christian, for you, is best understood as a state of mind. You made a decision to follow Jesus and, by whatever means, you are going to stick to it.

Why do I continue to live with the woman I married 33 years ago? The romantics will say that it's because I have grown to love her more and more every day, and that would be true. But actually, one of the reasons that is important to me is that I made a public commitment in front of witnesses to do something for better or worse 33 years ago, and, as a thinker, I intend to keep my word.

Do I occasionally find other women attractive? Yes, I do, but I made a promise. It is important to me to be a person of my word.

Whether you prefer love language or thinking language, try to love Jesus. Try to think Jesus. Spend time with the local people who want to do the same.

Pause for thought

You are living in God's world. Look around you and see what there is that is good. Enjoy the good things he has made and the good people he has put in different expressions of his church in your area.

Discussion questions

1. 'Love' language or 'thinking' language? Which motivates you? Which predominates at your church?
2. What are the best things about your local church? Would you take a friend to it if they did not share your faith?

Prayer

Lord, help me to rest and worship.

Introduction to Part 2

The Bible tells us to love our neighbours, and also to love our enemies;
probably because they are generally the same people.

G.K. Chesterton, *Illustrated London News*, 16 July 1910

Jesus takes the well-known 'golden rule' and turns it from positive to negative. It used to be said that whatever you don't want to happen to you, you shouldn't do to others. Indeed, Confucius said it.

So we should look out for the needs of others. They may look out for us, too, but that is not why we should do it. We should do it because we care.

What does all this say about our lives as Christians? We can be confident that the picture of a good father who made us, loves us and cares for us is a picture of a God who has our best interests at heart. Sometimes it is very difficult to see things from another's point of view. We feel we could do God's job better than he does. If you have ever felt like this, watch the movie *Bruce Almighty*, in which Jim Carrey's character gets the God job for a week while God goes on holiday.

If we feel that God has been remote and unspeaking, and if we are still asking, seeking and knocking, we should simply trust, wait and hope. If we want something to do in the meantime, we should find something good to do for someone else.

As we move on to the second part of the Ten Commandments, we become concerned with our relationship not with God but with each other. Ethics, in fact—plus courtesy, respect and neighbourliness, to name some close friends.

Campaigning in an election year in the UK, hear what the three main party leaders said about ethics:

Virtues come not from market forces but from our hearts.
GORDON BROWN, QUOTED IN *THE GUARDIAN*, 27 FEBRUARY 2010

Personal responsibility is the foundation of an ethical society.
DAVID CAMERON, SAME SOURCE

Unfairness is hardwired into our economy, politics and social lives.
NICK CLEGG, SAME SOURCE

We saw in the Introduction to Part 1 that Jesus summarised the Law, for the benefit of a questioner, as follows:

'Love the Lord your God with all your heart and with all your soul and with all your mind. This is the first and greatest commandment' (Matthew 22:37–38).

He then went on to say:

'And the second is like it: Love your neighbour as yourself. All the Law and the Prophets hang on these two command- ments' (vv. 39–40).

You do not have to relate to other people at all to keep the first part. But only with sacrificial love can you observe the second.

Part one of Jesus' answer is a quotation from Deutero- nomy. Part two is from Leviticus 19:18, so it too is an answer that comes from the Law, but is probably not so familiar a verse as his summary of part one.

'Which is the greatest commandment?' asks the expert. 'All of them,' says Jesus, in effect.

Jesus is saying that we should love God and love our neighbour. The rest is detail. In Luke 10, he is asked to qualify who should be considered a neighbour, perhaps because Leviticus 19:18 seems to be directed at those who might fall out with one of their own people. Jesus tells, in response, the great parable of the good Samaritan.

Judean Jews didn't get on with Samaritans. Their distrust dated back to the time when Israel split into two kingdoms, north and south. Your neighbour, Jesus says, is the most unlikely person you could possibly imagine.

The first part of Jesus' summary is probably well known, the second not so. But that doesn't make it wrong. It is later summarised in the letter of John:

For anyone who does not love his brother, whom he has seen, cannot love God, whom he has not seen (1 John 4:20b).

Loving others as much as we love ourselves and as much as we love God shows that our love for God is genuine.

Let's see how that might work itself out.

5

Those awkward other people

'Honour your father and your mother, as the Lord your God has commanded you, so that you may live long and that it may go well with you in the land the Lord your God is giving you.

Deuteronomy 5:16

It's easy to forget the fact, but in reality, most people are decent, honourable and kind. Most marriages don't end in divorce. Most people, in reality, love their immediate families unconditionally.

Philip Hensher, *The Independent*, 4 July 2003

Jesus described himself as the 'good shepherd' presumably to distinguish himself from some of the more disreputable 'hired hands' around at the time (John 10:11–12). Maybe we ought to describe God as the 'good Father': not everyone will have had a positive experience of parenting, and not all our images or memories of fatherhood will be good.

But many will be. As novelist Philip Hensher's words remind us, the media can give the impression that all is going wrong. In fact, 'children love their parents' is not deemed newsworthy because it's not unusual enough.

I have just been asked to comment on a newspaper statistic which said that 19 per cent (or, as the paper put, it 'one out of five') of marriages in our area involve one partner being unfaithful. I suggested that 'four out of five marriages are healthy' was clearly not the spin they were looking for.

We love to emphasise the negative in this country. Good news isn't news.

Let's get to honouring our parents, then. There is no short cut, as a Christian, to working on our behaviour with others and, from time to time, doing a bit of ethics.

If 'doing a bit of ethics' sounds like something you hoped you'd left behind at school, don't worry. We can do it slowly. But don't make the mistake of thinking you never want to get into it. Anyone who ever wondered if it was wrong to tell lies in all circumstances, always inappropriate for people of the same sex to have sexual intercourse, always wrong for a woman to have an abortion and never right to go to war—well, like it or not, you've taken an ethical position.

There is hope. As we consider the great leaders of the Bible, we have already noted in Chapter 2 that we come across some people whose ethics were a bit, well, dodgy. Moses the murderer, David the adulterer, Peter the liar—we talk of you again. Bad press. Yet God seems to be able to cope with failure. Clearly he likes holiness, but a spot of bad behaviour, really bad behaviour, doesn't invalidate a calling.

So we move on to the dizzy world of relationships. They'd always be fine if it wasn't for the other people. Other unique and special people. People made in the image of God but made, wait for it... slightly differently. So they see the world in a not-quite-the-same-as-me way—which can lead to minor disagreements, squabbles, friction, conflict, escalation of aggression, skirmishes, border disputes, suicide bombers, flying scheduled flights deliberately into buildings, and global thermo-nuclear war.

When my sons were very young, they often woke early and wanted something to eat before breakfast. On a day when my wife and I had the luxury of a lazy start and a coffee in bed, the parent on coffee-making duty would also bring upstairs a drink of juice for the boys and two small plastic bowls containing raisins. One bowl was yellow, the other green. I have no idea how it started but the green bowl was valued more highly than the yellow one. We had to try to remember whose turn it was to have the green bowl. Sometimes (and, if my sons read this, they will possibly be shocked and disappointed) I deliberately put extra raisins in the yellow bowl, simply as an experiment to see if it caused a reaction or made a difference.

Whenever bias was detected in a parent, one of the lads might utter the cry of the shortchanged child from down the ages: 'It's not fair.'

Over those early years with my sons, I came up with a mantra in reply: 'What do you want, a fair life or a fun one?'

I began to live in fear that they'd question how this might work out.

Go on, Dad. Define your terms.
Yeah. Tell us what you mean. How much fun is fair?

I stopped before they were old enough to do this, and they're way smarter than me now.

The good resides in the pressure to treat everyone fairly; the ill resides in the pressure to make everyone alike.
A.C. GRAYLING, THE MEANING OF THINGS (2001)

We do fall out with each other, and over the most ridiculous things, don't we? We invent rules to solve squabbles, but no rule in the world can legislate for our thought life. As comedian Al Murray's pub landlord character puts it:

The problem in the Middle East, in a nutshell, is this: lots of people living in a very small area who don't like each other very much.

Hopefully, being a Christian will change the way you see others. The rules place limits on our behaviour, but the principles are way stronger.

The late Douglas Adams' take on the gospel was this:

One man... nailed to a tree for saying how great it would be to be nice to people for a change...
THE HITCH-HIKER'S GUIDE TO THE GALAXY (1979)

Funny as Douglas Adams was, though, that is a hopeless underselling of Jesus' message. He called people to go so much further than being 'nice'. He called for sacrificial love, care and concern. Loving enemies. Going the second mile.

So why can't you get on with your mother?

Maybe, firstly, because the world of the commandment and today's world are separated by a lot of time.

Once upon a time, people lived in families and worked together—on the land, by and large. They farmed; they ate. It was the deal. Even in those communities that had not settled down and were foraging or nomadic, seeking pasture for their animals and wild food crops, the arrangement was the same. That is, until you got too old to farm or forage. Then the kids had to do it for you. So you had to rely on the children to feed you.

This is why 'Honour your father and mother...' is followed by 'so that you may live long...' If you expect your children to look after you when you are old, they need to learn how. They will learn by example if they see you looking after your own parents towards the end of life. You prolong their days; your days get prolonged. It's a virtuous circle.

Today, honouring one's parents is a little different. To start with, we don't live in a society that respects age. One change of attitude you might develop as you grow as a Christian is to look again at those people who are considerably older than you, to see them not as a nuisance but as a source of experience, life skills and personal history.

As we get older, we are able to look back on more and more of our lives. One of the problems with this is that older people tend not to take giant strides in discovery or invention because they don't take as many risks as the young. The old know of the dangers, the failures, the problems; the young have no idea, so they plough ahead. It is why so many young drivers take corners too fast and skid off the road; it is why some old folk drive frustratingly slowly.

I was talking with a group of young adults recently and they were amazed that when I first started work in 1973, in a large insurance office, there were no computers on any desks. We chatted about what life was like without mobile phones. I have to admit to having a sudden realisation of what it was like to be my gran when I quizzed her mercilessly about life in the early part of the 20th century. I also realised that in some people's eyes I was old. Curses.

So what resources will God give us to make the necessary

changes in order to step up to the mark in parental relationships?

The fruit of the Spirit is love, joy, peace, patience, kindness, goodness, faithfulness, gentleness and self-control (Galatians 5:22–23a).

If you have turned your life over to Jesus and asked for his Holy Spirit to invade your very being, then this list of delights is yours for the taking. The people God calls, he will equip. He will not ask you to begin (if it is a beginning) to see your parents in a new way without giving you help and support.

Many people embarking on the Christian life find a new joy in exercising patience. A new delight in showing compassion. A new freedom in discovering generosity. It is simply because they are getting in touch with the person they are meant to be. And, regardless of the desire to offer others the gift of eternal life, it stands to reason that the more people behave like this in the world, the better the world will be. Generosity is demanding today because too few people take it seriously, but the more the people who share the wealth, the less demanding sharing wealth becomes.

Unilateral behaviour (I do something for you before you do anything for me) is always costly.

Some cultures do not have old people's homes. They think it anathema that we shut our elderly people away from the family. My wife and I were guests at a Hindu wedding a few years back. As part of the after-dinner speeches, the three oldest ladies in the room were asked to stand, and they were applauded as a mark of respect. They were not praised for any achievement save that of living longer than the other female occupants of the room. Hindu families can be gathered from a wide area, so it was possible that this might be the last time some of these women were present with the whole family. I thought it was a terrific thing to do.

On holiday in Gozo (a less-visited island next to Malta), we were sitting in a village square bar, having a drink and reading. It was a Sunday and all the folk were gathered outdoors. A Catholic mass had just finished. A souped-up saloon screeched to a halt. As we watched what we thought was a young man's attempt to show off, we saw him get out of the car, engine running, run over the square to an old woman, kiss her and then get back in the car. You can be cool and show affection to your gran in public. They are not contradictory.

Now I know you didn't choose the family you were born into. Some of your relatives may drive you up the wall (and you them?).

Your mother may be overbearing, your father overprotective. If you are young, you want independence. Your parents want you to move out and stay in touch. One observation I have is that too few families talk through how this is all going to feel and what expectations the parents and children will have of each other once they are physically separated.

I hate the line in the carol 'Once in royal David's city' that throws an unbiblical Jesus at naughty kids, saying:

Christian children all must be
Mild, obedient, good as he.

The evidence for Jesus' mildness is flimsy. He grew up to throw tables over in the temple, of all places.

The commandment is addressed to children and chooses the interesting word 'honour'. Showing honour means showing appropriate and due respect—like what I saw at that Hindu wedding.

In the New Testament, we are offered an instruction to everyone to get all family relationships right:

Wives, submit to your husbands... (Ephesians 5:22)
Husbands, love your wives... (5:25)
Children, obey your parents... (6:1)
Fathers, do not exasperate your children... (6:4a)

Ephesians even has something to say to slaves and masters (6:5–9)—thankfully, an arrangement that is long past, but it's a reminder that everyone in the household has a relationship with everyone else, which is to be respected.

In each case it is assumed, or stated, that the relationship is 'in the Lord'. It is possible that the demands of your family and your faith will not concur. Then you will have to make a difficult judgment.

Places of relationship are places of pressure. At work, school or college, you find yourself in relationships that, unless you are the recruiter, you didn't choose. Ask yourself not how you can change the others, but what it is like for them to be in relationship with you. Do you take your turn to make the coffee in that open-plan office? Do you ask others how they are when you see them on Monday morning? Is it fun for them to spend time with you, or demanding?

Do you call your mother? (Excuse me, I must call my mother. Oh, she's fine, thanks for asking.)

As a witness to Jesus, do tell your story. If your behaviour is interesting, though, you may get asked to tell it. Ask others their opinions first. Ask others to tell their stories. Ask others how they make sense of the world. Keep going on this process of 'positive deconstruction' (Nick Pollard coined this term in his book *Evangelism Made Slightly Less Difficult*, 2004) until you get people to the point where they are dissatisfied with their worldview and want to know about yours. Have patience.

There is a whole new world of relationships that has come our way recently, which is the world of new social media. 'Following' people used to get you into trouble, but on a site such as twitter.com it is welcomed.

Exercise incredible caution before meeting people you only know through the Internet—not all is as it seems to be in the virtual world. But the Internet is simply space where people relate to one another, and Christians should be in that space and talking.

I have met one person I encountered through a website. After a few months of exchanging views, we met in a café in a large town and neither of us turned out to be a groomer or stalker.

When the commandment about honouring parents was written down, family groups were together, all the time. No one went off to college. No one moved out of town for a job. No child had to leave because they couldn't afford to own a home in their parents' village because second home owners had driven up the prices.

We live in a different world today. Very different. We all need to work out how to honour our parents. It may be a struggle, but we need to do it.

We also need to respect those older people around us who are more like an extended family would have been in the days of the Middle Bronze Age. Do you see the other people in your street that way? Perhaps you should.

Here's a story to finish the chapter. A young woman joined

an Alpha course recently at my church. Towards the end, she shared that she had loved talking to and mixing with the older people (our age range on this course was 19–78). She said that, having had a few bad experiences at school, she didn't find it particularly easy to relate to the young people at our church.

Has it ever occurred to you how few organisations there are that truly enable age barriers to be crossed? If you are relatively young, consider making your Christian service and worship at a church where folk are older. They will probably welcome you, love you and teach you.

Older people may grumble a bit, but who doesn't? Honour them. Then, one day, a young person may come along and honour you.

Pause for thought

Your home made you the person you are today. Is that a cause for thanksgiving, a matter for counselling or, as it is for many of us, somewhere in between?

Discussion questions

1. What do you want to happen to you as you get old?
2. Have you been honouring your parents?
3. What are the most difficult relationships in which you are involved? Why do they cause problems? Could you do anything about it?

Prayer

Lord, you were born into an earthly family; help us all to respect and honour the members of our own families.

6

Killing questions

You shall not murder.
Deuteronomy 5:17

Vengeance is a lazy form of grief.
Silvia Broome, played by Nicole Kidman in the movie *The Interpreter* (2005)

I do not imagine for a moment that I am writing to many murderers. I suspect that readers of this book are not, with malice aforethought, planning to do someone in. The positive way to state this rule is to say, 'Live your life genuinely wanting the best for other people.' There may be some people, this side of heaven, you find it difficult to like. That's fair enough, but you need to love them. That means wanting the best for them even if a colossal change would be needed before you got on well with them. In the meantime, the bottom line is, don't kill them. OK?

In fact, it is better to be nice to each other than nasty. Can I prove that? How about this:

- If you want generous birthday presents, give them.
- If you want lots of invites out, invite lots in.
- If you want to be called when you're ill, call when someone is ill.

- If you want to receive great communication, make sure you communicate well.
- If you want more love, give your love.
- If you want better facilities at your church, give time and money.

That doesn't say much about your motives, but I think it is true that a generosity of heart and spirit towards people will have its blessings. It is nice to be liked.

I am about to take the funeral of a recluse, a woman who lived alone and neglected herself and her family for many years. The mourners will be the undertaker, her daughter, her social worker, her solicitor and me. That service will be followed by the funeral of a former churchwarden, a much-loved man, ripe in years and most of them spent in Christian service. The church will be packed.

The former funeral will be especially sad because the churches in my town are full of people with helping skills, visiting skills and caring skills. I have met some fantastic people in the three and a half years I have lived in Nailsea. They are people who understand, as the Old Testament philosopher put it, that:

Two are better than one, because they have a good return for their work: if they fall down, one can help the other up. But pity those who fall and have no friend to help them up (Ecclesiastes 4:9–10).

The Bible does not want humans to be lonely, solitary creatures. We will see more about this in the next chapter. Loneliness was the first thing that God declared 'not good' (Genesis 2:18).

At your funeral, if people say you never hurt anyone, or you kept yourself to yourself, it will demonstrate that you weren't making enough effort to keep the rule of loving your neighbour as yourself. You want something to happen to you? Do it to others.

Actually, it's worse than that. If, at your funeral, the best they can say about you is that you kept yourself to yourself, then there won't be many mourners. No one will miss you.

Your life as a Christian really ought to have a new social setting. The business of doing to others what you would like them to do to you puts you in contact with the rest of the world, looking out for them, caring for them, wanting the best for them.

During the threatened pandemic of swine flu, we were all urged to have 'flu buddies'. We needed to find someone to go and get our prescriptions, to save taking our infectious germs out into the public sphere, if we got the flu. I think Christians should be at the front end of this sort of work and see it as a ministry. If you live near anyone who is elderly, or lonely for any reason, they should be able to rely on you. Make a difference in your neighbourhood. Be the person to go to when good is needed. It's a long way from 'Do not murder.' It is the polar opposite.

I live on a modern estate where people tend to keep themselves to themselves. During the cold winter of 2010, experiencing the shared hardship of being snowed in, a huge contingent of people, after three days of being stuck indoors, got out on to the street to clear the paths and roads. One or two people stayed 'on duty' for a lot of the worst days, looking out for vehicles in difficulty and coming out to help.

Shared hardship. Funny how it pulls us all together. Many older people talk longingly of the sense of community spirit and pulling together that existed in the UK during the Second World War. It took a mass of killing and destruction to generate comradeship.

What would it be like if Christians chose to look out for other people's needs when there was no hardship, just because that is the sort of thing we do?

Yet, to observe the aggressive, angry, frustrated people we encounter day by day, there must be something tragically wrong. Why do we become so intolerant when we get behind the wheel of a car or the guidance system of a supermarket trolley? Do people genuinely think that 'me first' is a more reliable route to a happy life than 'after you'? You would think that 'Do not murder' had become the only rule, all stops short of it being acceptable.

People tell me I am a patient person. I have many faults but I do manage to stay calm and not rush things, by and large. The opposite of patience is not impatience but anger.

At a large supermarket in Arnold in Nottingham, the car park, in the 1980s, was on the rooftop. It was above the store. You had no idea how full the car park would be without driving up the ramp to find out. The biggest frustration of my life, when doing the weekly shop, was to drive up the ramp in a procession of cars, only to discover that the car park had become full and the queue of traffic to get in now reached back to the ramp. The ramp was too narrow to allow a U-turn, so, if there was a car behind, there was no alternative. You were there for the duration. You had to wait for a space to appear. It could take a long time.

I resolved one day on the ramp, when I was particularly stewed about something, that I would simply observe, listen, and enjoy my car radio and the space to think. I can't begin to explain how many ideas for sermons I had from that day on in the queue. Problems got solved. Projects were hatched. My blood pressure went down.

There have been several changes in my life since then, one of which is to shop daily rather than weekly and to do it on foot if at all possible. That way, I maximise the number of people I bump into. It is better pastorally. I also keep fit.

It is wonderful, though, to enjoy the thinking time provided by a late visitor, a traffic jam or a delayed train. You can't do anything about it, so why not settle down into it? Certainly don't harbour resentment against someone who jumps the queue. Let them in with a cheerful wave, pray for them and give thanks for your more enlightened approach to life. If you feel the need to challenge their behaviour, do it generously, quietly and politely and be prepared to lose, even if you're right. It will be good for you.

As Jesus taught a crowd on a hillside, he did what all rabbis did in those days. He interpreted the law. He applied it to the lives of his hearers:

'You have heard that it was said to the people long ago, "Do not murder, and anyone who murders will be subject to judgment." But I tell you that anyone who is angry with a brother or sister will be subject to judgment' (Matthew 5:21–22).

Jesus went on to explain that if you were offering a gift at an altar, and remembered that you'd had a disagreement with another person, it was appropriate to make peace with that person before continuing. That is one of the origins of 'Sharing the peace', which is part of many acts of public worship today.

Recently I made an innocent joke in light conversation. It was at the expense of someone else, but we were all having a laugh and I had been the victim of several put-downs, too. I thought nothing of it. A few hours later, one of the people came up to me and told me they were deeply offended—so angry that they had wanted to hit me.

I apologised, of course, but became very sad that here was a relationship where I would have to be careful what I said all the time in future. I wouldn't be able to let my guard down. I'm a bit quick-witted and spontaneous in conversation. I sometimes say things to see how they will sound without especially meaning them. I give a straight answer to a straight question very quickly. My guiding principle is that I must do to others what I wish to be done to me, and I don't mind friendly joking like that.

I need to learn this: 'Everyone should be quick to listen, slow to speak...' (James 1:19)—even though it may compromise what I laughingly know as the essential me. But others might need to learn the next bit: '... and slow to become angry, for human anger does not bring about the righteous life that God desires' (vv. 19–20).

Is occasional accidental insensitivity the tax you pay on wit, or should all of us be taking a deep breath before speaking? Answers on a postcard...

The one key part of the answer, I think, is that we must try to assume the best motives in others. If someone does offend us, assume it was an accident. Allow them a slip of the tongue, an unfortunate turn of phrase or a joke at your expense. Anger disposal gets harder, the longer you leave the fuse ticking.

Someone I know sent an email to a church small group coordinator. She got an immediate reply, including one of the worst four-letter words. Instead of assuming that it was a hack or someone hijacking an email account, she withdrew from the group and brought the matter of this grave offence to my attention.

Naturally, there was an innocent explanation. I knew there would be. I knew the group coordinator pretty well. Small group leaders in my church tend not to tell their members, randomly, to do what this person had been told to do. That leader will always log off public computers carefully in future. But what a lot of fuss can be avoided if we assume that people are not out to get us all the time.

The interesting thing about my angry friend who had wanted to hit me was that, a few days later, in a different context, another member of the same family told me that they had been so cross with some contributors to the discussion in a meeting, they had wanted to hit them. I'm not sure that level of anger is genetic, but it can be learned in the family.

So what about anger management? From time to time today, we read of celebrities or sports stars being sent to anger management classes. In the recent past, they have included footballer Joey Barton and pop star Amy Winehouse.

The first-century Roman philosopher Seneca taught that a good dose of pessimism at the start of a day will help you cope. He lived at a time when the expectation for a dissenting philosopher, or Christian, was death in an unpleasant manner. He argued that if you chose to imagine such a death actually happening to you, then any day when it did not happen had turned out well.

Call me weird, but I find it helps me cope better if, as she comes through the door, I imagine that my wife has had a terrible day at work and is exhausted. If that really is the case, nothing is lost and I am ready to offer support (and red wine). If her day has exceeded my expectations, then I find myself feeling really happy for her.

Being a lifelong West Bromwich Albion follower has left me with a tremendous capacity for disappointment. I also found this a useful skill (disappointment, not Baggies supporting) in 27 years as both a volunteer and a paid youth worker.

Today we see road rage—the consequence of an over-optimistic view of other drivers. If we have a model of perfection in our heads, believing that road users will always drive or behave perfectly, then we are bound to be disappointed. If we allow motorists the freedom to be as human, mistake-ridden and clumsy as we can be on a bad day, they will probably disappoint us less.

One of the keys to anger management, then, is to lower our expectations of other people. That is not to say we should not trust others. Of course we should, but we should try not to be too disappointed when they let us down.

Another key is to have an outlet for anger. Some people use sports as such an outlet, hitting a ball rather than a person. Some play an instrument... or chop vegetables.

Should Christians be pacifists? I don't think so. There is a 'just war' theory. If you want to check it out, look at http://en.wikipedia.org/wiki/Just_War.

There is a time for sticking up for yourself. I have never hit anyone in my life, apart from in the playground as a small child. I am probably quite cowardly. I did smack my children when they were small but almost always regretted it afterwards and stopped when they were relatively young. I started losing fun fights with my older son when he was twelve. He was taller than me by 13, and remains so. Good company, though.

As a scrawny physical specimen at school, I developed the quick-wittedness to talk myself out of trouble. I reckoned that if I could make the aggressors laugh, I gained a moment to run away. It still works for me. It's turned into a knack for placating the angry on the phone, settling crying babies and talking down those who have lost their tempers.

I've also just realised (I'm a slow learner) that, psychologically, my quick-witted put-downs probably stem from a desire not to be bullied. I'm off for counselling.

If someone is behaving aggressively towards you (this advice will be needed mainly by men), try to avoid touch. It will only escalate a conflict to the 'Get your hands off me' stage. I made that mistake once. Never again.

Continue to look up to the church planter who didn't even see imprisonment as a hindrance to his preaching. Paul said:

Now I want you to know, brothers and sisters, that what has happened to me has really served to advance the gospel. As a result, it has become clear throughout the whole palace guard and to everyone else that I am in chains for Christ (Philippians 1:12–13).

Later, Paul wrote of the example of Jesus. The prophet Isaiah had foreseen a suffering servant:

He was pierced for our transgressions, he was crushed for our iniquities; the punishment that brought us peace was upon him, and by his wounds we are healed (Isaiah 53:5).

Paul said of Jesus:

And being found in appearance as a human being, he humbled himself and became obedient to death—even death on a cross! (Philippians 2:8).

As we come to the end of thinking about a command not to murder, we do well to recall that the death of Jesus Christ—a murder, some might say—is the answer to everything in the world that makes no apparent sense. The answer to death. The answer to suffering. The answer to evil. Thanks be to God.

It is good not to be a doormat Christian on whom everyone wipes their feet. Sticking up for yourself is not a bad thing. Doing it with truth and humility is a difficult skill to learn. Do try not to be more aggressive in emails than you are face-to-face. Don't bully people when you are on the phone rather than in their office. Try hard to be pleasant to those who work in call centres—it's a tough job. Reject cold callers with courtesy. Keep your text-life calm. Avoid Facebook or Twitter rage.

That sound hard? OK, go back to the top. Don't murder anyone.

Pause for thought

We all have different levels of violence in our lives. Take stock of yours.

Discussion questions

1. Do you ever want to hit people? What do you do when that happens?
2. How easy do you find James' advice about being slow to anger? What steps can you take to move in that direction?

Prayer

Lord, help me to see others as you see me. Help me to do to others as I would wish to be done by. Help me to love unconditionally.

7

Sexy stuff

You shall not commit adultery.
Deuteronomy 5:18

I don't know how long it takes to become a virgin again, but I think I'm halfway there.
Pamela Anderson, quoted in *The Observer*, 5 October 2003

Bad news, Pammy. You'll never get there. Your virginity, once you have given it away, is gone. You can't have it back. You can repent and make a new start but you can only ever have sexual intercourse for the first time once. Your virginity is a fantastic gift to give to your husband or wife. You can't go backwards.

Sex is brilliant, a great idea, and there is a clear biblical command to do it, right at the start of the Bible. More on being fruitful and multiplying later. God's oversight of the evolutionary process has taken us, over the years, to a place where those creatures that derive the most pleasure from sex will be most likely to breed. Clever. We don't need a biblical command to desire sex. It's built in.

Sex is powerful:

Sex carries within it the power of life itself. It is not an isolated act with no consequences. There is always the possibility that human history will be significantly altered by what this man and this woman are about to do.

ROB BELL, *SEX GOD* (2007)

There can be no doubt that sex for reproduction and sex for pleasure can both be life-changing. Giving your body wholly, unreservedly and without precaution to another person carries a load of risks, wonders and possibilities.

I heard this story some time ago but can no longer attribute it. Two monks were walking along a path when they saw an attractive woman trying to cross a stream but terrified of the water. The older of the two monks went over to her and, after a few words, raised her on to his back and carried her over the stream.

The two monks went on their way and, after a while, the younger monk asked, 'Brother, we are holy men who have made vows of chastity. Why did you touch that beautiful girl?'

'I have made the same vows,' said the older monk. 'I left her at the side of the stream. Are you still carrying her?'

With something so serious at stake as a new life, beginning with a furtive glance across a room or a piggyback over a stream, it is not surprising that sexual relationships are dynamite. They have a massive capacity to go wrong, and yet, when part of a complete commitment of one partner to another and used properly, sex is uniquely relationship-enhancing.

So the story of the monks reminds us that chastity is not a bad thing, just a difficult lifestyle choice to maintain. The Bible tells us that sex is a good thing, but that doesn't mean affairs, adultery and prostitution are good. Sex is a good thing when it's in the right place.

As I write, it's been John Terry, Tiger Woods, Ashley Cole and Iris Robinson who have been having their sex in the wrong place discussed publicly. By the time you read this, pound to a penny, there will be other names on the roll-call of promise breakers.

For those in the spotlight, the public apology often follows a private misdemeanour. From King David's post-adultery psalm, we read:

Against you, you only, have I sinned and done what is evil in your sight (Psalm 51:4a).

Of course, his adulterous partner Bathsheba's husband, Uriah, whose death David later arranged, might have felt somewhat sinned against, too. Sin spreads down the ages to Tiger Woods' public statement after many affairs:

I had affairs. It was not acceptable and I'm the only person to blame. I don't get to play by different rules.
TIGER WOODS, QUOTED IN *THE GUARDIAN*, 20 FEBRUARY 2010

Sex is a basic human instinct. We're designed to be sexually attracted to each other, and serial monogamy appears to have become the default setting for many people in 21st-century Britain.

Life is sex and sex is sin,
Come on, baby, let's begin.
THE DAN REED NETWORK, 'LIFE IS SEX', 1991

The Bible introduces checks and balances to sexual relationships. It eventually (for the Bible has a developing understanding of relationships over its pages, as we will see) identifies the correct place for sex as in an exclusive relationship. It condemns 'sexual immorality' (although it's never utterly clear about what that expression means). It condemns prostitution. It states that adultery is wrong. It calls for submission and love between husband and wife. It suggests that leaders will be judged by higher standards of sexual morality than others. It disapproves of divorce, while living with its occasional necessity.

But why, apparently, do churches have so much to say about sex, an essentially private activity? Probably because people are fascinated by what we have to say. The world does not sing from a single hymn sheet when it comes to sexual morality. *The Sun* newspaper's problem page and its sexual dilemma advice in cartoon form seem geared to the idea that we should only have a relationship with one partner at a time. Elsewhere, though, you will find adverts for chat lines that might suggest something quite different. The main pages of the paper will not be critical of a three-in-a-bed romp if all parties were consenting and adult.

It should not surprise us, then, that church folk do not seem able to agree what the message is. These questions will not be answered by all Christians with one voice.

- Is divorce wrong?
- Is premarital sex wrong?
- Is sex with a partner of the same gender wrong?

So, once again, we find that there is no short cut to thinking things through, reading our Bibles, discussing with others and prayerfully making our own judgment.

To answer these questions, we need to go back to the world in which the seventh commandment was forged. To repeat: if we think that the Bible gives a clear message about sexual relationships, we make a mistake. In the pages of the Bible we see a developing understanding. We easily fall into the trap of reading our own prejudices and preconceptions back into the text. Let's rewind.

In Genesis, the first thing we hear described by God as 'not good' is loneliness:

The Lord God said, 'It is not good for the man to be alone. I will make a helper suitable for him.' (Genesis 2:18)

I can now imagine any female readers demanding a retraction. 'Women are not put on this earth to help men,' they will say—and they're right. For the moment, though, we live with the truth that companionship is better than loneliness.

There are two parallel accounts of creation in Genesis. In 1:1—2:3, male and female are made simultaneously:

So God created human beings in his own image, in the image of God he created them; male and female he created them (Genesis 1:27).

In 2:4–25, there is a more poetic account, with the story of the woman being made from Adam's rib.

These words were, however, written in a time when a woman was deemed to be the property of a man. In the tenth commandment, the first thing we are told not to covet is 'your neighbour's wife... or anything that belongs to your neighbour' (Deuteronomy 5:21).

By the time of King Solomon, a man born out of a

relationship that began adulterously, the Bible sees nothing unusual in a king having 700 wives and 300 concubines. In fact, the Bible is only critical about the fact that these women turned Solomon's attention towards foreign gods.

The prophet Hosea, in a metaphor for God's relationship with Israel, is told:

Go, take to yourself an adulterous wife and children of unfaithfulness (Hosea 1:2).

This is a different world from ours. Writing to Timothy, Paul says:

Now the overseer must be above reproach, the husband of but one wife (1 Timothy 3:2).

This suggests to us a developing biblical understanding and a higher standard for leaders than for those being led. Others might have more than one wife, but not leaders.

We live in a world where some people feel that the Bible's literal teaching makes civil partnerships (legal relationships between couples of the same gender) wrong. Others feel comfortable with the thought that there are 2000–3000 years of cultural change between us and the Bible and that what is important is lifelong commitment, to the exclusion of all others. Either way, we have to respect each other and live together, celebrating the whole beautiful mess of *eros* and *agapé* (two Greek words for love, one generally considered to mean sexual love and the other Christian mutual support with self-sacrifice) that so fills up our senses, yet is still seen only dimly. One day we will see it with perfect clarity.

I truly believe that one day, in eternity, someone in the heavenly realms will offer me a drink that is so beautiful, so wonderful, that it will be the culmination of all my attempts to drink every real ale in the land, seeking 'the one'. Currently, it's Butcombe Gold. If your tipple is wine, or if you seek the perfect pasta, steak or cake, something similiar may happen to you.

The same applies to relationships, which is why Jesus told a questioner that he had misunderstood heaven if he thought there would be marriage there. There will be something in the afterlife that makes us realise what we were looking for in these human relationships—something wonderful, even compared to the heights that they can reach in our earthly life.

Are same-sex relationships wrong in all circumstances? I have decided that I will not tell anyone my view on this. I cannot, without upsetting some of my friends.

I understand that some people feel so strongly about this issue that they believe it is worth splitting the Church over. I don't. I am prepared to welcome same-sex couples to my church. I am prepared to condemn adultery and to condemn sex without commitment. I will not condemn gay people.

Sex outside a context of trust and permanence—as in casual sex or adultery—is the art of telling lies. It is saying physically what I could never say in words: 'I commit myself to you absolutely, permanently, vulnerably.'

MIKE STARKEY, *GOD, SEX & GENERATION X* (1997)

There is a very modern way of reading the Bible. By 'modern', I mean in relation to the last 300–400 years. For many years before that, Bible reading was corporate. It was read to people who couldn't read for themselves. It was, therefore, largely read in company.

Individual, private Bible study (no bad thing in itself) has not always been possible for the vast majority of Jesus' followers. While accessing the Bible's truth for ourselves is a wonderful thing to do, the escalation of privacy in Bible study has had one dangerous consequence. We never let the Bible surprise us. Instead, we try to surprise it. We live our lives full of our own prejudices, belief systems and ethical codes, and we try to read them back into the Bible.

So what happens when we get to a passage such as this?

'You have heard that it was said, "Do not commit adultery." But I tell you that anyone who looks at a woman lustfully has already committed adultery with her in his heart' (Matthew 5:27–28).

The answer is, we don't let it strike us afresh, as Jesus' hearers would have had to, but we come to it full of a whole barrowload of stuff that we 'know' for ourselves.

The first thing to notice, of course, is that Jesus is speaking to men. It is a man's 'look' that is condemned.

Reading the wider context, we see that Jesus has been preaching on the Law. He is expounding it for his contemporary audience. 'Don't murder' has become 'Don't get angry.' A desire for revenge to be appropriate, rather than excessive, has been reinterpreted as 'Love your enemy.' Now he suggests the removal of eyes if they cause you to commit adultery, and the chopping off of similarly naughty hands.

We make the mistake of thinking that this passage condemns lust and condemns divorce but doesn't advocate eye removal or hand chopping, unless we allow the scripture to surprise us.

The Archbishop of Canterbury reminds us that we have to work hard at applying scripture to our lives:

It is not... magical text, supernaturally giving us guaranteed information about everything under the sun.

ARCHBISHOP ROWAN WILLIAMS, *TOKENS OF TRUST* (2007)

Jesus says, 'You have heard it said'—not 'It is written' (although it is, even on the walls of many old churches, behind the sanctuary), but 'You have heard it said.' Clearly, the things people were saying at this time were important. Most people then heard the law spoken. They did not read it for themselves.

Matthew is writing his Gospel to a group of Jews who had seen their capital city fall and their temple destroyed, and were grinding out a living in the wilderness around Jerusalem in the late first century. He quotes Jesus as saying:

'Do not think that I have come to abolish the Law or the Prophets; I have not come to abolish them but to fulfil them. I tell you the truth, until heaven and earth disappear, not the smallest letter, not the least stroke of a pen, will by any means disappear from the Law until everything is accomplished' (Matthew 5:17–18).

People are being reminded by the teachers of the law that adultery is still out. The commandments still apply. In full.

What is adultery? The Oxford English Dictionary tells us that it is 'voluntary sexual intercourse between a married person and a person who is not their husband or wife.' 'Do not commit adultery' is, therefore, a minimum standard. It could mean that every sort of pursuit of gratification with someone who is not your husband or wife, short of penetrative sex, might be legal. But Jesus thinks otherwise.

A story will illustrate the point.

A rich woman was interviewing candidates to be her chauffeur. One of her occasional journeys would involve driving along a narrow road on the edge of a steep drop.

'How close,' the woman asked, 'would you be able to drive to the edge of the cliff and guarantee my safety?'

The first applicant assured her that, within a metre of the edge of the cliff, she would be quite safe.

The second had more confidence in his own ability and suggested but a few centimetres from the edge. He would know the boundary clearly enough, for he was very experienced.

The third applicant, a stern woman with a great CV, simply looked the employer in the eye and said, 'Madam, I would try to keep you as far away from the edges of cliffs as possible.'

She got the job.

Jesus, in this sequence of sayings in Matthew, takes several 'You have heard it saids' and reminds us each time of a more demanding standard: 'You have heard it said... but I say to you...'. The Law stops you at a barrier at the end of a slippery slope. Jesus' interpretations suggest avoiding the slope altogether. He recommends that you drive a long way from the edge... or he would if he had heard of cars.

Let me show you what some of the scholars say about Jesus' teaching:

It is not merely the act that is condemned, but the attitude from which it comes. Deliberately to foster lust, by erotic books, plays, films, magazines and websites, is to fly in the face of this commandment. For who is to know when the bridle of decency or convention will snap under the strain, and the racehorse of our passions break loose?

MICHAEL GREEN, *THE MESSAGE OF MATTHEW* (2000)

Adultery is but the final expression of lustful thoughts har-boured in the imagination and fed by the illicit contemplation of the object of desire, so that the lust of the eyes and the lust of the flesh cannot be disassociated.

R.V.G. TASKER, *MATTHEW* (1971)

Just as the control of anger will prevent murder, resisting lust at the stage of thought and desire is the prophylactic recommended by Jesus against adultery.

GEZA VERMES, *THE AUTHENTIC GOSPEL OF JESUS* (2004)

Here is one modern secular commentator:

Adultery is now a quaintly old-fashioned descriptive term, used by churchmen and other judgmental moralists. It is not a breach of a moral code, or even a defining constant within marriage. Spouses who commit adultery are no longer considered to have undertaken an act that is contradictory to the spirit of the publicly celebrated relationship.

DEBORAH ORR, *THE INDEPENDENT*, 31 MAY 2006

So what should we say? Adultery takes two. Long before Jesus, the world knew this:

See that no woman commits fornication with her eyes or her heart.

THE BOOK OF JUBILEES 20:4

We must also note that Jesus is clearly using hyperbole (de-liberate exaggeration) in this series of statements. You agree. You probably still have both your eyes and both your hands. It is, however, an exaggeration sandwich. Earlier he suggested

95

that the result of not settling your debts with your adversary, regardless of who is right, may be prison until you pay the last penny (Matthew 5:25–26). So when Jesus tells us we have committed adultery in our hearts, is he exaggerating? Sex might have been our first thought ('I want some of that'), but did we actually go as far as adultery? Well, was sex our second thought, too?

Here it gets a bit vulnerable. I'm a bloke. I'm designed and built to notice that which I personally find physically attractive. And here's the problem when people say to me, 'Don't look at women lustfully.' There isn't a huge amount of thinking time between the words 'look' and 'lustfully'. It isn't a 'Hmm, I wonder' timeframe. I'm not waiting in the supermarket queue (as I was the other day), carefully calculating and reminding myself that the way I just looked at that woman at checkout 9 was lustful. I just look for a bit longer than usual, because I'm made that way. Nice curves.

Now, after a bit, all sorts of checks and balances cut in. She's wearing a wedding ring. Oh yes, so am I. I have made promises to someone else. I don't want to jeopardise those promises. Adultery is wrong. I praise God in my heart for her beauty and nothing further happens. I can still visualise her if I try, but the picture is fading and would have gone completely if it wasn't for this book—so I put it to you that it's all your fault.

Here's what I think Jesus is saying. He's saying that 'lustfully' is how men look at women. We need to be aware of that and let it go no further. No further. Wherever we find ourselves on the slippery slope towards adultery, the answer's the same:

1. If you have looked at the other, married person and have approached him/her to start a conversation... Back off.
2. If you get into a conversation and walk out talking... Say goodbye and walk the other way.
3. If you agree to go for a coffee... Drink quickly and leave.
4. If you exchange numbers... Don't call. Delete it.
5. If you agree to meet again in private... Don't show. If you are alone in a room... Make excuses and leave.
6. If you have exchanged knowing glances and some saliva... Stop and leave.
7. If you are naked and excited... Stick your own fingernail firmly into your own inner thigh, scream, jump into a cold shower, dress and leave.

The nearer the cliff edge you drive, the more likely it is going to be that you plummet. Jesus knew that. He thought stopping was important. More important than entering heaven with all your body parts in this world of exaggeration.

Don't suffer too much guilt, though, if an attractive member of the opposite sex makes you look for a moment longer than strictly necessary. It's not a design fault. According to Genesis, the first thing God said to humans was:

'Be fruitful and increase in number; fill the earth and subdue it' (Genesis 1:28a).

It's a euphemism. He said, 'Get bonking.' We ought not to be surprised that there are some mechanisms built into creation to make obedience to that command more, not less, likely.

We can sound all prudish by reeling off some of the slogans of modern chastity. 'True love waits.' Well yes, it does, but that comes over as negative, not positive. Our virginity ought to be too precious a thing to give away lightly. We should, if we can, be enthusiastic about friendship, companionship and *agapé* before *eros* gets a look in.

If you are worried about whether, at your marriage, you and your partner will be sexually compatible, and you're wondering if you should have had a test drive before you bought the vehicle, don't worry. There can be no more delightful thing than two inexperienced lovers teaching each other what to do, what they enjoy and how to give and receive pleasure. It may take a little while. Your partner is a person, not a car, anyway.

If things have gone wrong for you, repentance is possible and so is forgiveness. God cannot give you your virginity back, but he can give you an 'as new' start.

The key to understanding all this is the idea of respect. I must see other human beings, with their desires and needs, as more than the solution to my sexual needs. If I respect you and I am not married to you, then having sex with you should be the last thing on my mind, not the first.

Pause for thought

I am fearfully and wonderfully made in the image of God.

Discussion questions

1. What (or who) are you still carrying that you should have left at the side of some river somewhere?
2. Which of the fruits of the Spirit—love, joy, peace, patience, kindness, goodness, faithfulness, gentleness or self-control—is of most use in one-to-one, potentially sexual relationships?

Prayer

Give thanks for the gift of sexuality and pray that you find, or continue to enjoy, an appropriate sexual relationship.

8

Honesty 1

You shall not steal.
Deuteronomy 5:19

You know you're in the Bible Belt when there are more prisons than Starbucks.
David Gale, played by Kevin Spacey in *The Life of David Gale* (2003)

Someone once told me that, although we regularly condemn our 'materialistic' society, our problem, as epitomised by litter and junk, is that we are not materialistic enough. I am beginning to understand what they meant. As an enthusiastic recycler, composter and giver away-er, I now say amen to that. More materialism, please—but in the sense of having less stuff and taking more care over the way we discard it.

This not-materialistic-enough society has seen to it that no one need ever buy:

- An elastic band: pick them up off the pavement after a postal round.
- Paper clips: they come as a free gift from many people who write to me enclosing more than one sheet of paper.

- Pens: they are sent in the post accompanying surveys I don't wish to fill in; occasionally, I am sent an engraved one with my name on it, as an example of the sort of thing I may wish to persuade my business to purchase in bulk and give away.
- Printer paper: much of the stuff I print off can be printed on the blank side of a used piece of paper.

I have also, relatively recently, tried to embrace minimalism. Less is more. I used to keep far too much stuff. Now, If I'm not going to read a book again, I pass it on. And if I use www.bookcrossing.com, I can follow its adventures around the world.

Getting rid of stuff to a good home can also be done through www.freecycle.org.

I enjoyed greatly the moment when my old upright piano went off to the home of a young lad who was about to embark on piano lessons. If it gave him half the pleasure it had given me, now the proud owner of a brand new piano, then it would be brilliant. It also saved his parents from investing in a piano until they knew how seriously he was going to take his lessons.

Give stuff away if you can.

My sister is a devoted minimalist. Often her flat will have only one thing of colour in the whole place, and no clutter. A single red tulip in a small vase on her dining-room table, in an otherwise bare room, draws so much more attention to the inherent beauty of that bloom that you wonder why anyone would ever want to display more than one at a time.

Sorry if I have just offended any church flower arrangers. They can produce terrific work but, on the whole, our churches are incredibly untidy and cluttered, and give the impression that everyone is scared to throw anything out in case it was donated in memory of someone else.

We have so much stuff that we have forgotten the value of the individual items. Things are nice. Things are valuable. Having too many dilutes their value.

About 15 years ago, a new Christian (we'll call him Ed) joined our home group. Knowing that I enjoyed music, he told me he had found a great way to get free music. He borrowed CDs from the library and copied them before returning them.

I don't want to stomp around in the music copyright minefield for now, but the thing that lives with me is the look on his face when he saw the look on our faces. He genuinely, really genuinely, had no inkling that what he was doing was wrong—that it was theft. He simply thought he was being smart.

That is what the law, in all its truth and beauty, is for. I don't believe Ed was sinning in the eyes of God. He had no idea that what he was doing was wrong as he did it. Ignorance may be no defence in law but, when confronted, he changed his ways. He repented.

When the letter to the Ephesians was written (scholars disagree, by the way, about whether it was actually written by Paul), it is clear that the church in Ephesus was having problems. You cannot read Ephesians 4 and imagine all was going well:

Put off falsehood and speak truthfully (v. 25).
Do not let the sun go down while you are still angry (v. 26).
He who has been stealing must steal no longer (v. 28).

Falsehood, anger and theft must have been going on or the letter would not have condemned them.

The problem was that the Christians in Ephesus were good at evangelism—so good that liars, angry people and thieves were being converted. That is the magic of the gospel. It is good news before it has any implications for behaviour. So this letter, with all the authority of apostleship, delivers a striking message: don't carry on as you were before.

The commandment is reaffirmed. Stealing is wrong.

For anyone who becomes a Christian today, there are discoveries to be made about behaviour related to theft.

The commandment is brief. It makes no distinction between a pencil and a person. In those days, a wife or child would have been seen as a man's property, which could be, potentially, stolen. The brevity is the genius. Scripture respects property. It also teaches that we should hang loose to possessions, knowing that our worth does not come from what we own. As Jesus said:

'Where your treasure is, there your heart will be also' (Matthew 6:21).

So what things might we accidentally steal? How about time, for instance? In the modern developed world, a lack of punctuality is considered to be stealing someone else's time.

How about supplies at work? Many people see their place of work as the place to go to top up their personal store of stationery or toilet rolls. They surf the net in company time. They see it as a right, a fringe benefit.

That essay you just wrote for a school assignment. Did it not lean rather too heavily on a work you found on the internet?

We have all done this. When I was at school I found myself, for reasons I cannot fully understand, studying economics. I had an essay to write and I copied it almost word for word out of the *Junior Pears Encyclopaedia*. My teacher made no comment on the obvious plagiarism but simply pointed out a couple of factual errors in the piece. I felt let down by the encyclopaedia. If a reference book couldn't get an A, what chance did I have? Fact is, though, that I knew no economics by the time I had finished the course. Passing off someone else's work as my own was theft. As I have worked on this text, I have tried to be careful to identify my sources, give credit for quotes or, at minimum, rework someone else's good ideas into my own words.

When I was 13, I went on a boating holiday with the family of a school friend of mine. The guy was a bit of a bully in those days and had greater physical stature than me (most people still do). On a trip to the shops one afternoon, he showed me a keyring he had stolen from a gift shop. He also told me that if I told anybody, he'd 'bost' me, a Brummie expression at the time for a good beating.

I was shocked. I was friends with a shoplifter, a thief. I hated that. Not yet a Christian, I had some under-the-surface moral values. A conscience. We all find that peer pressure gets to us, but at some point in most of our lives we look at our peers and realise they're not all that clever.

I don't know if I was too timid to be a thief, but I resolved, in as much as a 13-year-old can ever resolve anything, that this was not a lifestyle I wanted to copy.

To put this instruction bluntly, don't nick stuff. Even before you find it pronounced as wrong by the Bible and the law, it is still not worth it.

Are there more subtle temptations to steal? Music copyright is complicated these days. The gift of creativity in music is magical, and people who can do it, and do it well, deserve to receive reward.

I was quite critical, when it first began to happen, of the practice of sampling, especially when no credit was given to the original artist. They say that middle age is when you recognise no new songs but only the tunes that have been sampled. Today the practice is usually acknowledged and is recognised as an art form in its own right. Many contemporary songs use samples and improve dramatically on an original work. Not all, but many.

The thing that changed my mind about this issue was a *South Bank Show* episode called 'John Lennon's Juke Box'. You can still see it on Google videos at: http://video.google.com/videoplay?docid=-7532896021332831792#

Lennon, whom I greatly respected as an artist, lifted many of his ideas and riffs directly from the rock-and-roll or rhythm-and-blues songs that were around when he was a teenager. Listening to the interviews with some of the artists featured on the *South Bank Show*, you can tell that they are not upset by this, but flattered. This is the way music has always worked: one person's ideas become part of the working pattern of another.

Today, the creativity of the DJ is much respected, but most artists seem to insist on due credit being given when a sample is lifted, rather than being flattered.

For those of us who are ordinary 'punters' of the music business, it has never been easier to file-share or find ways to make a free download. With a new, Jesus-centred lifestyle, your first thought should not be about how you can gain something, but what, if anything, you are stealing from others. Is the artist who gave time and energy to make this music getting a reward for it? If it is their livelihood, are they actually making a living from it?

Whenever we steal a little because 'they won't miss it', we cause a little damage. We behave in a way that, if everyone did it, would be horrid.

Stealing one daffodil from a huge display won't make any obvious difference, but it is wrong. Taking one glass from a pub to finish our drink in the cab will cost the pub a little; if it happens often, it will cost a lot. We all pay a small bit extra for our goods to make up for those who shoplift. Shops don't call it theft; they call it 'wastage'.

Not repaying debt makes you a gradual thief; not returning borrowed items, likewise. They give you thief-like tendencies.

The Ephesian correspondence follows its instruction to thieves to steal no longer with the thought that the thief 'must work, doing something useful with his own hands' (Ephesians 4:28b).

So the counter to thieving is service. Get stuck in. Get your hands dirty. Serve your church. Serve others. If you were a bit of a servant before you became a Christian, you will find this easy. If you weren't, you will find that people begin to like you more. Jesus is our example:

[He] made himself nothing, taking the very nature of a servant (Philippians 2:7a).

Churches have a huge range of ministries—preaching, healing, worship leading, hospitality, youth and children's work and so on. You may feel you're not up to any of those, but don't forget that a huge range of other practical skills are required.

The church I lead meets in a school. Every Sunday morning, a team has to set up the hall, the chairs, the PA, the refreshments, the worship area, the musical instruments and the children's work—and take it down again afterwards.

One thing we have noticed at our church is that there is an excellent balance of genders, whereas many churches report more women than men. It may be that having lots of small practical jobs to do on a Sunday keeps our male attendees happy.

If you are a new Christian, ask your church leaders how you can help practically. If you throw yourself into it, you will have no time or energy left for theft, even if you feel 'called' to it.

The verse about the reformed thief goes on: '... that he may have something to share with those in need' (Ephesians 4:28b).

A thief makes people poorer. This is a strong underlying theme of the Bible's witness, from the law:

If there is a poor man among your brothers in any of the towns of the land that the Lord your God is giving you, do not be hardhearted or tightfisted toward your poor brother (Deuteronomy 15:7).

The passage goes on to suggest that loans are better than charity but debts should be cancelled every seven years, a principle that many argue should be taken into politics today when dealing with developing nations.

If we turn to the prophets, we read:

For three sins of Israel, even for four, I will not turn back my wrath. They sell the righteous for silver, and the needy for a pair of sandals. They trample on the heads of the poor as upon the dust of the ground and deny justice to the oppressed (Amos 2:6–7a).

Amos condemned people for making treks to shrines while being unfair in the marketplace, for worshipping God with their lips but not letting him make any difference in their lives.

If you are to be known as a Christian, it has to make you different. Has to.

If we go to the Gospels, we find the words of Jesus:

'When you give to the needy, do not announce it with trumpets, as the hypocrites do' (Matthew 6:2a).

Jesus continued the theme, but suggested that care for the poor was not to be done to glamorise the giver but should be carried out without seeking credit. Will you be nice to people when nobody is looking?

In the early church, we find another example to point us in the right direction:

In Joppa there was a disciple named Tabitha… who was always doing good and helping the poor (Acts 9:36).

Elsewhere, in the New Testament letters, we are told to 'continue to remember the poor (Galatians 2:10a).

The generosity of the wealthy helps the less well-off to keep the eighth commandment. All of us would probably, if we're honest, try to get away with an act of theft to feed our hungry children, if there was no alternative. We must look after the poor before they are put in such a situation.

Do not steal; help others not to.

Pause for thought

Generosity is helping others not to steal.

Discussion questions

1. Does this chapter cause you difficulty in any areas of your life where you might have compromised the commandment?
2. How materialistic do you think you are?

Prayer

Lord, help me to value the material gifts of this world as you do and use them in your service wherever possible.

9

Honesty 2

You shall not give false testimony against your neighbour.
Deuteronomy 5:20

Always tell the truth; that way you don't have to remember what you said.
Mark Twain, *Mark Twain's Notebook*, 1935

Strange that, in the way language gets mangled, 'God's truth' has become the colloquial, semi-swear '(God) Strewth'.

What is false testimony? What is God's truth?

I don't know about you, but I like blunt people. I like the company of folk who will ask clear questions, give an honest opinion when asked, not look round for compliments all the time and not worry if their words have offended. Such people sharpen me. I hate it when I am surrounded by people-pleasers who only want to say what they think I want to hear. Hate it. Ironically, it doesn't please me. More to the point, I think they are giving false testimony.

I have always been like this myself and have had to be taught the skills of tact, diplomacy and timing over the years (not very successfully). Nevertheless, I still walk into many pastoral situations wondering if I dare say what I actually think.

In effect, the only two interview questions I find of any use when seeking a colleague are, 'I am blunt; will that be all right?' and 'Will you be clear and straight with me, too?'

It may surprise you to learn that, in some cultures, truth is not the highest value. In many African cultures, you will find family valued higher than truth. Offering a promotion to your brother or sister instead of a stranger would not be considered out of order but would be expected. People don't feel they are sinning if they promote a relative over a more deserving candidate. Traditional British culture finds that wrong.

In many Eastern cultures, honour is prized more highly than truth. So, rather than admitting failure, a person might contemplate suicide. Traditional British culture finds such an idea horrific.

In most English-speaking cultures, truth is rated above all.

Our politicians have found many ways of avoiding the sentence 'I lied.' For a while in the 1980s, lying was known as being 'economical with the truth'—or, in one famous instance, being 'economic with the *actualité*'. Don't you love the idea that, somehow, speaking in French offers more clarity? More *gravitas*, anybody?

A parliamentarian might get away with an affair but will never survive lying to the House of Commons about it. Several politicians have had to leave high office over the years because of this.

In case you feel it is obvious that truth should be put on a pedestal, let me describe a scenario to you. You are sitting in a room with your loved ones. A gun-wielding stranger bursts in. He asks, 'Is <insert name of your loved one> here?' It looks pretty much as if it will be curtains for the named person. Would not the thought of a lie cross your mind? In fact, is it not incredibly likely that you will lie if you think it will save someone you care for greatly? Living has a higher value than truth on some occasions, then.

If a man came to my front door brandishing a gun, my wife answered and the man said, 'Does Steve Tilley live here?' I rather hope she might find it in her soul to lie—a bit.

Perhaps one day in the future, when Christians find themselves under terrible oppression and persecution, you will be asked to identify yourself as a Christian and face death for so doing. Might you lie?

You would be in good company:

As Simon Peter stood warming himself, he was asked, 'You are not one of his disciples, are you?' He denied it, saying, 'I am not' (John 18:25).

Mark's Gospel tells us that this lie led Peter to break down and weep. He had failed to identify himself with Jesus and felt terrible about it.

This prompts us to assess whether we feel as bad as we should, if we fail to identify ourselves with Jesus when an opportunity presents itself.

In the days when the 'false testimony' commandment was crafted, it was possible to cause someone's death by giving false evidence against them in court. Many crimes in those days carried the death penalty. The law makes absolute the need for courts to be places of integrity. This is still the case today, and someone giving evidence in court will be asked to swear an oath of honesty.

The commandment is so non-specific that all acts of untruthfulness stand condemned—white lies, exaggeration, false claims on a CV, agreements to do things simply to please people, with no intention of seeing the action through, and, of course, political manifestos. Not for nothing is it said, 'We campaign in poetry; we govern in prose' (New York Governor Mario Cuomo, 1985).

What is 'campaigning in poetry', though, if not setting out false expectations?

I was telling a story to a friend. It was a good story but it wasn't about something that had happened to me. It was a tale I had heard from someone else's lips. Then I realised I was telling it as if I had been involved personally. Rather than carrying on, I stopped myself and apologised. My friend, a good and kind individual, said, 'Don't worry. The narrative demanded it at that point.'

It was nice of him. When we claim credit for things other people did, when we tell stories with ourselves as the star when we were not, or when we exaggerate for effect—even if it is clearly a dramatic device—we still, in effect, lie. The narrative may have demanded it at that point but, if we didn't explain that that was what was happening, we lied.

I often explain, when I'm leading discipleship groups, that coming to terms with religious language is a necessity. In fact, coming to terms with language generally is an important skill for a Christian. So much of our faith is about words. Narrative devices in books, plays and films may not necessarily be the clear, scientific truth but may be metaphorical truth.

You might say of a gardener, 'She has green fingers.' You might say to a late date, 'I've been waiting here for ages.'

Neither statement is a lie, but it's not scientific truth, either. Usually the context will explain what we are doing. Again, we must remind ourselves to be aware what kind of truth we are dealing with when we're using religious language. What sort of 'son' is Jesus? What sort of 'father' is God? What sort of 'comforter' is the Holy Spirit?

The context of the parables in the Gospels warns us that Jesus used works of fiction to make a point. So an expert in the law asked Jesus, 'And who is my neighbour?'

In reply Jesus said: 'A man was going down from Jerusalem to Jericho…' (Luke 10:29b–30a).

We do not read the missing words, 'Once upon a time', but we understand them. We know that this is going to be a story.

When UK Prime Minister, Margaret Thatcher, famously said that no one would have remembered the good Samaritan if he hadn't had money, she was blurring the edges between history and story. It was a bit like saying that no one would have remembered Luke Skywalker if he hadn't owned a lightsabre. The parable of the good Samaritan was a story that Jesus made up and told to make a point about neighbourliness. It was not a lie. It was a story containing truth. (Maybe the government needed to stop passing by on the other side?)

What about you? I don't know if you have reached this point of Christian commitment with a reputation for honesty that you can continue to carry with you into your Christian life. It is the easiest way—however blunt you may end up being.

Mark Twain's advice quoted at the beginning of this chapter is still valid. If you tell the truth, it is easier to recall what you've said.

This is a mantra that the late DJ John Peel repeated endlessly. He had a quaint habit of self-deprecation for one in the public limelight. It may have been why so many people liked him so much and why he appealed to generation after generation of music lovers. He never worried that telling the truth against himself might do him harm. He figured it was easier to be laughed at now for being honest than to be rubbished later for being a liar.

Lies often have to be covered by other lies, then helped out by further lies. Soon the lies have tied you up so tightly that you end up hoping two people, to whom you have told two different lies, never meet to compare notes.

If you have come to faith from a past in which lies have regularly fallen from your lips, I am afraid that, having met the one who is the truth, you are probably going to have to work on a new script.

I encourage you to pray, with the psalmist:

Send forth your light and your truth, let them guide me; let them bring me to your holy mountain, to the place where you dwell (Psalm 43:3).

As a young curate, I was once seeking a prayer to pray from the pulpit before preaching a challenging sermon that contained an element of rebuke for the congregation. A wise woman whom I trusted showed me a prayer she had copied from the wall of a church in Jersey on holiday:

May I open my lips to speak the truth.
If it is the truth, may it be the whole truth.
If it is the whole truth, may it not be merciless.

I like the balancing act required of the preacher as implied in that prayer. Total truth with mercy.

As well as valuing truth, though, our society values tact, discretion and diplomacy. How are you going to answer the question, 'Does my belly look big in this?' Does it make a difference if his belly looks big in everything?

I know it won't work for every marriage, but if my wife tries something on that doesn't suit her, I tell her so. Firstly, it is the truth (although I do make it clear that it's only my opinion). Secondly, if I then say I really like something, she will know I mean it. Having a voice of constant encouragement in your ear can be debilitating. You end up asking yourself, 'Don't I ever do anything wrong?'

What about truth's neighbours and relatives?

Our family members are like us but different, too. It is amazing how many dilemmas are truth-related, so let me introduce you to some of truth's relatives.

- Hypocrisy is saying one thing but doing something else.
- Exaggeration is making the truth more interesting for the sake of our reputation.
- Being unreliable turns our promises into lies.

All three are bad.

Hypocrisy will get us into trouble and darken the image of God in us as seen by others.

Exaggeration tends to make us lack trust in our own story—and it escalates. If our exaggerated story still doesn't get a reaction, we may have to grow it some more.

Saying you will go somewhere and then not turning up, or that you will do something which doesn't get done, spoils your reputation and, if you are known as a Christian, spoils the reputation of Christians. You are like an employee of a large company, wearing a uniform. If you are known as an unreliable Christian, you make the church less accessible.

Ever noticed those signs on the back of large lorries? 'Driven courteously? Phone…'

Big organisations know that everything, right down to the way their lorries are driven, reflects on the company. A truck from a well-known retail chain sped down the high street the other day in the rain and soaked several of us pedestrians. I gladly tell others now. You never know the reach or impact of the people you upset. It's the same for Christians.

People are watching our light on the hill and our salt in society. They want to catch us out. I want to say that they may disagree with individual actions—not all Christians agree about everything—but they should never be able to challenge our motivation.

Tact, diplomacy and sensitivity are some other relatives of the truth. They involve not telling the truth for fear it might hurt someone. This can be good. We should reflect on the fact that tact, diplomacy and sensitivity are all loosely related to lies, yet we value them. One word of warning: if we are not careful, we can be so tactful that we never tell anyone the truth, in case it hurts their feelings.

A person who undertook much one-to-one ministry in a training capacity was once discussed in a meeting I attended, and a number of people agreed that he had a personal fresh-ness problem. We all pussyfooted around, but agreed that someone had to say something. Of course, nobody wanted to be the one actually to do it. Who would? Somehow, I know not why—perhaps I didn't put my hand down fast enough—the job fell to me. When I plucked up the courage to deliver the news, it was well received and did not spoil my relationship with the other person. And I think I want to say that if I ever have such a problem, I would want the first person who experiences it to tell me.

I encountered a similar situation recently, and a colleague of mine said, 'If no one tells her [it was a 'her' this time], then soon everyone in the church will know about it except her.' The truth may hurt but it is a helpful hurt.

It is not my natural inclination to be an encourager. I am good at remembering to thank people, but, not especially relying on the need for encouragement myself, I have to try hard to remember to do it. I am also more likely to spot the flaws in someone's performance than the flourishes.

A nice way to say 'thank you', in a world of texts, emails and word-processed form letters, is a handwritten postcard. I have a huge supply of cards in my desk drawer and enjoy matching the picture or image with the receiver, if possible. I can't tell you how much goodwill is caused by the simple act of posting a thank-you card.

We do not get called to make public promises much these days. Marriage, court cases and oaths of office are about the limit for most people. As a Christian minister in his fourth Anglican church job, I have probably done it more than most. New ministries are always marked by swearing an oath of allegiance to the Queen and to the Bishop of the diocese.

I don't actually like making promises. I find that being asked to 'promise' devalues the other things I say. I try (in the words of Jesus) to 'let my "yes" be "yes" and my "no", "no"' (Matthew 5:37). If I say I will do something (and write it down so that I don't forget), I usually do it or apologise/renegotiate. It means a lot to me to do what I say I will do.

The same goes for swearing on the Bible, which I have been asked to do only twice in my life—once in connection with a legal affidavit and another time when giving evidence in a courtroom. Why should placing my hand on the Bible change my attitude to the truth?

We should look forward to the day when we have no need of oaths.

We follow a Saviour who lost his temper in a temple, called his closest follower Satan, called a Samaritan woman a dog and remained silent at a trial when the truth might have saved his life.

There may be no room for compromise, but this truth thing is not as clear-cut as we think.

Let us recall our big promise—our big truth. Our one big promise, our key oath, is our commitment to follow Jesus. Baptism and confirmation in the Church of England involve several public pledges, including:

- I turn to Christ.
- I repent of my sins.
- I renounce evil.

Other truths to do with our behaviour flow, hopefully, from this. As Jesus said:

'Everyone who hears these words of mine and puts them into practice is like a wise man who built his house on the rock' (Matthew 7:24).

Let us build our lives on the rock of Jesus' words.

Pause for thought

We live our lives with more principles than simply 'Truth at all costs'. Mercy, grace, loyalty and honour are also in there somewhere. We need to weigh them up, too.

Discussion questions

1. In what circumstances are you most tempted to be dis-
    honest?
2. How would our public life change if all politicians told
    the whole truth all the time?

Prayer

*Lord, you are the way, the truth and the life. Help me to follow and
live honestly.*

10

You're all right, you are

You shall not covet your neighbour's wife. You shall not set your desire on your neighbour's house or land, his manservant or maidservant, his ox or donkey, or anything that belongs to your neighbour.
Deuteronomy 5:21

Happiness is not having what you want; it is wanting what you have.
Rabbi Hyman Schachtel

In March 2001, British artist Michael Landy took over a retail space on London's Oxford Street. Everything he owned, from his car to his clothes, was transported down a conveyor belt to an industrial-strength shredder. It was a work of art and a protest against consumerism.

Today's mantra is the opposite, which is why this performance artist made such a splash. We want more. More things. More power. More fame. 'I really want this' is the cry of the contestant on *Masterchef*, *Pop Idol* or any of a number of reality TV programmes.

We want to get better. We want to stand out. We want it through our own efforts.

The Bible's message is at odds with this. It says that we need to be content with who we are.

I worry that the desires of some reality TV contestants are hollow. They want fame. How it comes or what it is for don't seem to matter. In fact, many of them have not worked out what to do with the trappings of fame when fame comes knocking. A big bank account and a row of cameras trained on your doorstep. Is that what you want?

When I was 22 years old, I married and bought a house (with a staff mortgage from my then employer, an insurance company). Those sorts of offers are not easy to find now, and I acknowledge how fortunate I was.

What I do remember, as clearly as if it were only yesterday and not three decades back, is sitting in my lounge, looking at the walls and thinking, 'These are mine.' It was a remarkable feeling for one so young. I didn't want a mansion. I was delighted to have my own home. I was happy.

My happiness was related to possessions, though. I had some learning to do. These days, I own no property, have a pretty demanding job, and yet have probably never been more content. I believe I am in the place where I should be, doing the job I should be doing and trusting God for my financial future.

The idea, 'Don't worry; be happy' is a very alluring one. That said, it is hard to get to the point where you feel you have all you need. Most people don't want a lottery win. The majority feel that 'a little bit more' is all it would take to make them satisfied.

Even that thought, given that most people want better things not just for themselves but for their families, too, is not unnatural or disgraceful.

Many people find that becoming a Christian gives them a new joy, a new contentment. It is satisfaction at a deeper level than anything they have ever known before.

But not all do. Some make the step of faith as an intellectual assertion but notice no emotional difference. Others, almost grudgingly, come inside the kingdom with a bag full of questions and continue asking them. Still others simply decide that you can do more damage to a machine by being a piece of grit in it than by throwing rocks at it from the outside. So they step inside the church machine and try to change it.

How do you reach contentment?

Many tricks can be played. You can compare yourself with the number of people in the world who have to live on less than $1 a day. Now you feel wealthy.

You can compare yourself with those who are sick, suffering or persecuted. Now you feel at an advantage—although there is a school of Christianity that takes an 'If it isn't hurting, it can't be Jesus' approach to life.

A few weeks ago, I began making a note in my diary each day to do with my health. What, if anything, had been wrong with me physically that day? It was amazing. In the first three months of 2010, I had only 15 days without some minor ailment. The things wrong were small and pathetic—mouth ulcers, a bit of eczema, a twisted knee for a few days. Most of us go through life like this.

I asked the members of a small discipleship group to score their current state of health on a scale of 1 to 10, where 1 = very unwell and 10 = perfect health. Most of the group of twelve or so people scored between 6 and 8.

If you have a mouth ulcer, be content. If you have a bit of eczema, be content. These things are normal.

The main problem that has affected my health during my life is a double anneural tear (two slipped discs), which left me in pain and discomfort for several years. After good advice, and no surgery, from a neurosurgeon, I learnt that although my back hurt, exercise was causing no further injury. So, if I exercised through the pain, I would get better.

I did. It was hell, but it worked. Every day since then (the last bit of back pain was seven years ago), I have rejoiced at the simple ability to stand up for a while without sciatic pain, and at the luxury of a slow walk, which used to be terribly uncomfortable. I would have accepted a disabled sticker. I got fixed—and now I appreciate that fact so much more. As Joni Mitchell said:

You don't know what you've got till it's gone.
JONI MITCHELL, 'BIG YELLOW TAXI'

One day there will be a Revelation 21 moment:

'He will wipe every tear from their eyes. There will be no more death or mourning or crying or pain, for the old order of things has passed away' (Revelation 21:4).

In the meantime, God provides the daily miracle of health care, nurses and doctors, dentists, paracetamol, antidepressants, cough mixture and soothing balms, to name but... however many that was. Enjoy.

What about wanting more money?

Author Richard Foster, in his book *Money, Sex and Power* (1987), suggests that every now and again it is good to cash your salary cheque, lay the money out on the floor and look at it. Whatever your net salary is per month, you probably never see it. On the first day, standing orders and direct debits for mortgage, insurance, pension and council tax take their chunks. You have other budgeted needs. But look at that money and say to yourself, 'What would I do if I had that much?' It is an exercise in reminding yourself that you are wealthy.

There is a 'part two' to the exercise. Christians believe that we are merely stewards of the earth. God put us here to look after it. He said:

Fill the earth and subdue it. Rule over... every living creature' (Genesis 1:28).

As we examine our money, we can remind ourselves that it is all a loan from God. Job understood this principle:

'Naked I came from my mother's womb, and naked I will depart. The Lord gave and the Lord has taken away; may the name of the Lord be praised' (Job 1:21).

God has put us in charge of a small amount of the world he has made. Money is our way of ruling. We do well to remind ourselves that it is God's earth, God's rule, and we are temporary trustees. If you like, it is his money.

Now, do you still want to lust after next door's Mazda? It 'exudes Japanese sports car performance and is the perfect definition of Zoom-Zoom' (www.mazda.co.uk).

Oh, you do? Wouldn't it be better to give thanks for its graceful lines and beauty without lusting after it—a technique that we discussed as being handy in resisting the next-door neighbour's wife or husband, too?

Or maybe you lack contentment with your appearance:

A poll on women's body shapes found 55% of girls want to change the size or shape of their assets.
MYFACEMYBODY.COM, QUOTED IN *THE SUN*, 22 MARCH 2010

I've had times when it was hard for me to look at myself in the mirror, because I didn't really like who I was.

SUPERMODEL NAOMI CAMPBELL, QUOTED IN *THE SUN*, 22 MARCH 2010

Men's sense of inadequacy can be played on, too. I imagine such fears are rife out there, given the number of offers I get in my email inbox to increase the length or girth of my penis. Presumably some people respond to this stuff or it wouldn't be worth sending.

Jesus said:

'Therefore I tell you, do not worry about your life, what you will eat or drink; or about your body, what you will wear. Is not... the body more important than clothes?' (Matthew 6:25).

Oh dear. He's on clothes now. It's a raw nerve for the Christian community, whose meetings Peter Owen Jones once famously described as 'the annual dinner and dance of the synthetic fibres association' (*Bed of Nails*, 1996).

It can look as if our avoidance of covetousness has led to an avoidance of caring for ourselves. Loving others as we love ourselves includes the idea that we should love ourselves.

It is true that fashion is both a cultural issue and a tremendous drain on our resources if we insist on looking 'on trend'. I like my clothes. I probably spend more than most men on them. There are areas of my life on which I spend less than most. We all have to make decisions about what we do with our disposable income. But the commandment wants us to avoid wanting things simply because our neighbour has them, and Jesus wants such things not to be the cause of anxiety. He doesn't say, 'Don't plan' or 'Don't budget'. He says, 'Don't worry.'

I think the dress sense of the Christian community might well be an area that could reasonably be invested in, with a little more planning and budgeting. If we have learned anything from modern advertising, it is that poor presentation will let us down. Can we improve, while avoiding the opposite extreme of having to have the latest fashions and discarding perfectly usable clothes after one season only? Let's try.

What we look like is our presentation of ourselves, made in the image of God, to the outside world.

It is the subject of ridicule by many:

You may dress like a Christian but there the similarity ends.
PATSY, *ABSOLUTELY FABULOUS*

I think the gay community has much to offer the church—dress sense, for one thing.
THE REVD RICHARD COLES, RADIO 4 PRESENTER ON *SATURDAY LIVE*

Fashion is an instant cultural response to changing times. So is music. It is easier to respond to cultural trends with three metres of fabric or three chords than with thousands of tons of concrete and glass. So architecture lags behind a bit.

What is 'culture', anyway? I have never found a better definition than Brian Eno's: 'Everything you don't have to do.'

Thus, eating is not culture, but cuisine is. Clothes are not culture, but fashion is, and so on.

This means that our purchasing behaviour is also our cultural behaviour. When we collect music, art or even shoes, we are making a cultural statement. The third millennium is a complicated time for avoiding covetousness. Much of our talk about wealth creation can mean 'sell more things'. We don't want to, er... buy into that. But we must be aware that the artist, the musician and the fashion designer are all humans with mouths to feed. They are doing their best. As with much of this sort of stuff, it is a balancing act.

Eat a pizza. Surf the Internet. Watch telly on your phone. You do that long enough and you don't notice the neighbourhood falling to pieces around you. People roll over. And if you get fat, you're easier to roll.

Before I identify the source of that quote, take a moment to digest it. Here is someone saying that laziness, materialism and living in a virtual reality will lead you to fail to register discontent with the outside world.

Who said that? Stand up, 1970s anarchist-in-chief, Sex Pistol Johnny Rotten, now working as John Lydon, interviewed in Q magazine, April 2010.

We need to work on being content with what we've got, yet willing to make things better for others. Obviously no one lives with completely pure motives, all the time. Campaigning for something that will make your town nicer/safer/better will also make your life nicer/safer/better.

As I said at the beginning of Chapter 8, I think that there are two problems with our materialistic society. First, we are too materialistic. We have too much stuff. Chucking out, recycling, freecycling, taking to a charity shop and living with less are all tremendously liberating. Beginning to embrace minimalism, I find that I appreciate my possessions much more for having fewer of them lying around. But we are also insufficiently materialistic. So our society has devised things that are replaced rather than repaired. We get a new iron, toaster or lamp if the old one breaks. Litter is the consequence of a society that doesn't look after and tidy away its small things.

Covetousness is a cancer. It eats away at us. It leads us to debt (if we buy things we can't afford) or theft (if we simply take them).

The Bible knew this. At a time when a previously nomadic community was starting to settle down, it is likely that differences between farming abilities, the quality of the land or the size of the family workforce meant that there was usually a neighbour somewhere who was doing better than you. What this commandment is saying to us is that a slight difference in wealth between people is normal.

American author and broadcaster Garrison Keillor describes his imaginary town of Lake Wobegon as a place where all the children are above average. Such a statement summarises all our hopes and aspirations but also shines a light on our stupidity. We can't all be 'above average', and if we are not all the same, we should not covet.

We live in a competitive world. I am quite competitive. I have personal bests for walking to the shops and back. I sometimes allow others' success to spur me on to success. If a colleague preaches a good sermon, I want to preach a better one. I use my lack of satisfaction with not being the best to make me better, but I try to stop short of wishing my colleagues would do worse. I applaud ability with words and I am glad when they speak well.

Rick Warren, the American pastor behind the *Purpose Driven* series of books and resources, uses such a method to keep himself working hard. He says, 'No one is going to outserve me.'

That idea may be useful for some of us, but remembering that we are 'human beings, not human doings' is equally important.

A colleague going on sabbatical leave a few years ago told

me that he was going to try to devote himself to being rather than doing. He then presented me with a list of all the things he was going to achieve during the following three months, to this end. To be a better father, he was going to make sure he collected his kids from school. To be a better husband, he was going to make sure he allocated one evening a week to spending alone with his wife.

Becoming content with who you are is a change of mindset, not a thing to put on your 'to do' list.

So how do you become content? It is a bit of a cliché, but the Christian journey you are now on is a marathon, not a sprint. Hopefully, you are now a Christian and willing to serve Jesus all your days. At the end of Matthew's Gospel, there is a 'to do' list and it has a key proviso. We are not alone in this task:

'Go and make disciples of all nations, baptising them in the name of the Father and of the Son and of the Holy Spirit, and teaching them to obey everything I have commanded you. And surely I am with you always, to the very end of the age' (Matthew 28:19–20).

Jesus is with us. That's amazing and powerful. That makes it his work, not ours, and, best of all, it means that the results of anything we do in his name are down to him. It shouldn't make us lazy, but it should take the pressure off.

What happens when things go wrong? If we have slipped into covetousness?

I think it comes back to self-understanding. At the centre of the idea of coveting is the feeling that we do not like ourselves. Yet God made us, unique and special:

You made [us] a little lower than the heavenly beings and crowned [us] with glory and honour (Psalm 8:5).

Who am I? If I am not happy with the answer and wish I was someone else, then I need to ask one of the questions that Moses asked God in Exodus 3 and listen to the answer:

Moses said to God, 'Who am I, that I should go to Pharaoh and bring the Israelites out of Egypt?' And God said, 'I will be with you' (Exodus 3:11–12a).

It's the same answer as Jesus gave his disciples in the 'great commission' in Matthew 28. 'I will be with you.' It should be good enough.

Pause for thought

What do you own? If you cashed in all your property, how would you feel? How much cash would you have?

Discussion questions

1. Imagine you have been campaigning for a better fire station in your town, and then plans are drawn up to build a new one next to your house. Now how do you feel? This may not sound like a question about covetousness, but it is designed to explore the difference between 'I want' and 'We want'. Are you prepared to accept some minor personal disadvantage for the sake of the good of the community, or do you covet a quiet life?
2. What is your identity? Think about all the different ways you could answer the question, 'Who am I?'

Prayer

Lord, help me to view my possessions as the equipment you have provided to enable me to worship and serve you.

Conclusion

I'd like a banner over my church, house—indeed, life. It would say:

QUESTIONS WELCOME HERE

I have made it a life's work to ask questions and, if I have succeeded, this book will have raised more of them than it has answered.

I believe that asking questions is brilliant. Everyone has something to teach us. Just find the right questions. Everyone is an expert on something. They may not realise it, but just find the right questions to ask them.

Telling people your opinions might start a conversation, but only if you are interesting. Asking someone else's opinion will always start a conversation. Furthermore, you can gently nudge opinion by asking questions.

There is something slightly strange about the Old Testament people of God and their commandments. They valued, almost to a ridiculous extent, the fact that they had 'the law'. They carried it around with them. They made an ornate container for it. They eventually built a temple to house it. They lost it and then ripped their clothes in anguish when they rediscovered it and realised they had forgotten it. They made up rules to help them keep the rules. It is almost as if they were proud to have more boundaries than other peoples. Almost? No. Precisely. These people believed that God had revealed himself to them more intimately, more completely—more, yes, appropriately—than to any other people at any other time in history.

Christians believe they were right to believe it. The revelation had not yet come to completeness—it took the gospel to bring it there—but it was new, dramatic and life-changing. Worth valuing. For us, it is worth exploring and understanding; it's an agreed starting point, if you like, for talking about faith.

Following Jesus is about relationship, not rules. Mustard seed shavings are not a fragment from a rule book but the smallest bit of a small bit of faith.

I have always been interested in conversion. I am particularly interested because I didn't have a moment of conversion myself. Over a four-year period, I moved from being outside to inside the Christian community. There were key steps and people on the way but, actually, conversion is something I have to allow to happen to me every day.

It is tough. Twenty-six years ordained and I still go one year at a time, recommitting myself, privately, at Easter each year.

Somewhere along the way, I will sing this hymn, a song with lyrics so beautiful that almost none of the many tunes to which it is sung have been able to spoil it.

When I survey the wondrous cross
On which the Prince of Glory died;
My richest gain I count but loss,
And pour contempt on all my pride.

Forbid it, Lord, that I should boast,
Save in the death of Christ, my God;
All the vain things that charm me most,
I sacrifice them to his blood.

See, from his head, his hands, his feet,
Sorrow and love flow mingled down.
Did e'er such love and sorrow meet,
Or thorns compose so rich a crown?

Were the whole realm of nature mine,
That were an offering far too small;
Love so amazing, so divine,
Demands my soul, my life, my all.
ISAAC WATTS

Demands my all. Indeed it did—and still does. No half-measures. All or bust.

I hope this book has helped you on your journey. I'd love to hear your comments, through Twitter or via the publishers.

How do you teach someone to be a Christian in the 21st century? You teach them to believe and trust in the Lord Jesus Christ.

How do you teach them to go on being a Christian in the 21st century? Same answer as to the first question.

Thank you for reading.

Come and See

Learning from the life of Peter

Stephen Cottrell

When we look at the life of Peter—fisherman, disciple, leader of the Church—we find somebody who responded wholeheartedly to the call to 'come and see'. Come and meet Jesus, come and follow him, come and find your life being transformed. This book focuses on Peter, not because he is the best-known of Jesus' friends, nor the most loyal, but because he shows us what being a disciple of Jesus is actually like. Like us, he takes a step of faith and then flounders, and needs the saving touch of God to continue becoming the person he was created to be.

Come and See, first published as *On This Rock*, is also designed to help you begin to develop a pattern of Bible reading, reflection and prayer. Twenty-eight readings, arranged in four sections, offer short passages from the story of Peter, plus comment and questions for personal response or group discussion.

ISBN 978 1 84101 843 0   UK £6.99
Available from your local Christian bookshop or, in case of difficulty, direct from BRF using the order form on page 143. You may also visit www.brfonline.org.uk.

Bible Reading: a beginner's guide

Michael Green

The Bible may be the bestselling book in the world, but reading it—let alone understanding and applying it to daily life—can be a daunting prospect even for people who feel they are some way along the road of Christian discipleship. Where do we start? How do we work out its relevance to us? If we feel we know it quite well already, how can we go further in exploring its riches?

This highly accessible book sets out straightforward and helpful strategies for those who are completely new to Bible reading, as well as those who have begun to develop a Bible reading habit and want to broaden and deepen their understanding. Step by step, Michael Green explains how to enjoy the Bible (and avoid feeling bored by it), how to read it by ourselves and benefit from discussing it with others, and how we in turn can start to share its teaching with new Christians.

ISBN 978 1 84101 610 8   UK £4.99
Available from your local Christian bookshop or, in case of difficulty, direct from BRF using the order form on page 143. You may also visit www.brfonline.org.uk.

Prayer:
a beginner's guide

Jane Holloway

If prayer is simply a matter of talking to God, why do we often find it so difficult? While a surprisingly high percentage of people in the UK admit to praying at some time or other, the challenge for Christians is to move beyond prayer as crisis management or shopping list, and experience it as being in the very presence of our heavenly Father.

Jane Holloway has spent many years learning about prayer and encouraging others to do the same. *Prayer: a beginner's guide* offers a simple yet thought-provoking introduction to what prayer is and how it works, and includes many helpful suggestions for developing how and when we pray. Filled with up-to-date stories about the power of prayer from across the world, it will motivate, encourage and inspire the most hesitant pray-er. Each chapter ends with a selection of practical prayer exercises.

ISBN 978 1 84101 611 5   UK £4.99

Available from your local Christian bookshop or, in case of difficulty, direct from BRF using the order form on page 143. You may also visit www.brfonline.org.uk.

Running the Race Marked Out for Us

Lessons from Hebrews 12

Andrew Wooding Jones

While events such as the London Marathon grow in popularity year after year, with athletes training to beat their personal best and raise money for charity, the general assumption today is that when things get tough, it is much easier to give up than press on through the pain barrier. Persevering is not a popular idea—but that is exactly what God calls his followers to do, as this book spells out.

In a verse-by-verse exploration of one of the New Testament's most inspiring passages, this book invites us on the challenge of a lifetime—the race of faith, which we run in the company of a 'cloud of witnesses' who urge us on as we follow in the footsteps of Jesus. It reveals a wealth of encouragement and hope in Hebrews 12, and reminds us of all that we are called to do and be as sons and daughters of God.

ISBN 978 1 84101 527 9   UK £5.99
Available from your local Christian bookshop or, in case of difficulty, direct from BRF using the order form on page 143. You may also visit www.brfonline.org.uk.

One Dad
Encountering God

Brad Lincoln

What if God has left an important clue about his personality somewhere inside us, as if, in making us, he left his signature?

This book shares the reflections of one ordinary man about what it means to be a dad—and how that fits in with his feelings about life, the universe and God. If we are made in the image of our heavenly Father, we can learn a lot about what it means to be a dad through looking at what God is like. And reflecting on our relationship with our own children can help us begin to glimpse how God feels about us. *One Dad Encountering God* does not set out to provide all the answers but to get you thinking about what really matters in life.

ISBN 978 1 84101 678 8   UK £6.99
Available from your local Christian bookshop or, in case of diffi-culty, direct from BRF using the order form on page 143. You may also visit www.brfonline.org.uk.

Seeking Faith, Finding God

Getting to grips with questions of faith

John Rackley

What does it mean to be a disciple of Jesus, living according to his gospel today? Part of the challenge of following that path is how we communicate what we believe to friends, neighbours, colleagues and family members. But how do we explain ourselves to a society that is profoundly ignorant of God's revelation?

This book shows how our witness gains authenticity when we develop a seeking and searching faith. In five sections of reflections—A yearning faith; A gospel place; Gospel encounters; Faith companions; Praying the gospel—John Rackley wrestles with the challenge to develop such a faith and looks at what we can learn from those who first followed in Jesus' footsteps.

ISBN 978 1 84101 543 9   UK £6.99
Available from your local Christian bookshop or, in case of difficulty, direct from BRF using the order form on page 143. You may also visit www.brfonline.org.uk.

ORDERFORM

REF	TITLE	PRICE	QTY	TOTAL
843 0	Come and See	£6.99		
610 8	Bible Reading: a beginner's guide	£4.99		
611 5	Prayer: a beginner's guide	£4.99		
527 9	Running the Race Marked Out for Us	£5.99		
678 8	One Dad Encountering God	£6.99		
543 9	Seeking Faith, Finding God	£6.99		

POSTAGE AND PACKING CHARGES						
Order value	UK	Europe	Surface	Air Mail	Postage and packing	
£7.00 & under	£1.25	£3.00	£3.50	£5.50	Donation	
£7.10–£30.00	£2.25	£5.50	£6.50	£10.00	TOTAL	
Over £30.00	FREE	prices on request				

Name _____ Account Number _____

Address _____

_____ Postcode _____

Telephone Number_____

Email _____

Payment by: ❑ Cheque ❑ Mastercard ❑ Visa ❑ Postal Order ❑ Maestro

Card no ❑❑❑❑ ❑❑❑❑ ❑❑❑❑ ❑❑❑❑ ❑❑❑

Valid from ❑❑❑❑ Expires ❑❑❑❑ Issue no. ❑❑❑

Security code* ❑❑❑ *Last 3 digits on the reverse of the card.
ESSENTIAL IN ORDER TO PROCESS YOUR ORDER   Shaded boxes for Maestro use only

Signature _____ Date _____

All orders must be accompanied by the appropriate payment.

Please send your completed order form to:
BRF, 15 The Chambers, Vineyard, Abingdon OX14 3FE
Tel. 01865 319700 / Fax. 01865 319701 Email: enquiries@brf.org.uk

❑ Please send me further information about BRF publications.

Available from your local Christian bookshop.   BRF is a Registered Charity

About
brf:

BRF is a registered charity and also a limited company, and has been in existence since 1922. Through all that we do—producing resources, providing training, working face-to-face with adults and children, and via the web—we work to resource individuals and church communities in their Christian discipleship through the Bible, prayer and worship.

Our Barnabas children's team works with primary schools and churches to help children under 11, and the adults who work with them, to explore Christianity creatively and to bring the Bible alive.

To find out more about BRF and its core activities and ministries, visit:

www.brf.org.uk
www.brfonline.org.uk
www.barnabasinschools.org.uk
www.barnabasinchurches.org.uk
www.messychurch.org.uk
www.foundations21.org.uk

If you have any questions about BRF and our work, please email us at

enquiries@brf.org.uk